Rasputin

For Barbara

Pocket BIOGRAPHIES

Rasputin

HAROLD SHUKMAN

SUTTON PUBLISHING

First published in 1997 by
Sutton Publishing Limited · Phoenix Mill
Thrupp · Stroud · Gloucestershire · GL5 2BU

Copyright © Harold Shukman, 1997

British Library Cataloguing in Publication Data
A catalogue record for this book is available from the British
Library

ISBN 0-7509-1529-3

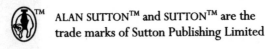

ALAN SUTTON™ and SUTTON™ are the
trade marks of Sutton Publishing Limited

Typeset in 13/18 pt Perpetua.
Typesetting and origination by
Sutton Publishing Limited
Printed in Great Britain by
The Guernsey Press Company Limited
Guernsey, Channel Islands.

CONTENTS

CHRONOLOGY

22 Jan. 1869	Birth of Gregory Yefimovich Rasputin in Pokrovskoe, Tobolsk Province, Siberia
1888 or 1889	Rasputin marries Praskovia Dubrovina
26 Nov. 1894	Nicholas marries Alix of Hesse
7 May 1896	Coronation of Nicholas II in Moscow
1901	Philippe Vachod, the French clairvoyant, introduced to empress
1903	Rasputin arrives in St Petersburg, returns to Siberia after five months
4 Feb. 1904	Outbreak of Russo-Japanese War
12 Aug. 1904	Birth of heir to the Russian throne, the Tsarevich Alexei
22 Jan. 1905	Bloody Sunday in St Petersburg
17 Feb. 1905	Grand Duke Sergei assassinated in Moscow
5 Sept. 1905	Russo-Japanese Peace Treaty of Portsmouth, New Hampshire
20 Oct. 1905	General strike
30 Oct. 1905	Nicholas II signs October Manifesto granting civil liberties
Autumn 1905	Anna Vyrubova introduced to Nicholas and Alexandra
14 Nov. 1905	Rasputin meets tsar and tsarina
10 May 1906	First State Duma opens

Chronology

21 July 1906	Duma dissolved
Nov. 1906	Rasputin treats tsarevich for first time
3 Mar. 1907	Second Duma opens
15 June 1907	Second Duma dissolved, new electoral law announced
20 Nov. 1907	Third Duma opens
Summer 1909	Rasputin and Father Iliodor tour monasteries and visit Pokrovskoe; Rasputin meets Prince Felix Yusupov
1910	Complaints about Rasputin by grand duchesses' governess
Mar. 1911	Prime Minister Stolypin sends Rasputin away from capital; Rasputin begins second pilgrimage to Jerusalem
14 Sept. 1911	Stolypin assassinated in Kiev
Dec. 1911	Church tribunal investigates charges against Rasputin
Jan. 1912	Prime Minister Kokovstev advises Rasputin to leave capital
28 Nov. 1912	Fourth, and last, Duma opens
1914	Rasputin meets Prince Andronnikov
Feb. 1914	Prince Felix Yusupov marries tsar's niece, Princess Irina
Spring 1914	Rasputin meets Dmitri Rubinstein
June 1914	Attempt on Rasputin's life by Chionya Guseva
1 Aug. 1914	Germany declares war on Russia
Sept. 1914	Rasputin returns to St Petersburg
Jan. 1915	War minister dismissed, spy mania spreads

Mar. 1915	Rasputin creates scandal at Yar Restaurant in Moscow, banished from capital; Princess Irina Yusupova gives birth to daughter
June 1915	Anti-German riots in Moscow; Yusupov's father dismissed with ignominy as governor-general
July 1915	Empress calls Rasputin back from Siberia; Rasputin urges tsar to take over supreme command
Aug. 1915	Press campaign against Rasputin
5 Sept. 1915	Tsar takes over supreme command from Grand Duke Nikolai; Scandal over canonization of John of Tobolsk
16 Sept. 1915	Duma prorogued
Nov. 1915	Rasputin secures appointment of Pitirim as Metropolitan of Petrograd
Feb. 1916	Goremykin replaced by Stuermer as prime minister
Nov. 1916	Duma reconvenes, Milyukov makes his 'treason or stupidity' speech
30 Dec. 1916	Rasputin murdered
4 Jan. 1917	Rasputin buried at Tsarskoe Selo
Mar. 1917	Riots in Petrograd; Provisional government formed; Nicholas abdicates, royal family placed under arrest; Rasputin's body exhumed and burnt
April 1917	Lenin arrives in Petrograd
July 1917	Kerensky becomes prime minister

Chronology

Aug. 1917	Royal family removed to Tobolsk, Siberia
7 Nov. 1917	Bolsheviks seize power
1918	Volunteer Army formed by anti-Bolshevik generals
Mar. 1918	Soviet–German Peace Treaty of Brest Litovsk ratified
May 1918	Royal family moved to Ekaterinburg
July 1918	Tsar's brother and other grand dukes murdered
29 July 1918	Royal family murdered by Bolsheviks

EARLY DAYS

The fall of an empire demands explanation in terms of historical forces that one expects to match the scale of the events themselves – major war, economic collapse, social revolution. But individuals also have their place. It is, for instance, impossible to think of the Russian revolution without mentioning Nicholas II, Kerensky, Lenin or Trotsky. Yet among these names we also invariably encounter that of Gregory Rasputin, usually described as a drunken, lecherous pseudo-holy man, a debauched peasant whose baneful influence over the Empress Alexandra was to prove fatal to the Romanov dynasty. A small private museum has been opened in his birthplace which aims to show that his reputation as an utterly amoral and mercenary reprobate is based mostly on myth. He has featured in novels and films – even in a pop song that opened with 'Ra, Ra, Rasputin/Lover of the Russian queen/Russia's greatest love machine'.

The purpose of this book is to identify the qualities that enabled Rasputin to enter Russian history, and that lent themselves to this sort of treatment, to ask what made the Romanov dynasty susceptible to his influence, and to explain why the relationship was ultimately disastrous.

We shall examine a number of related areas: the condition of Russia from the turn of the century to the First World War; the relationship between the tsar and society; religious attitudes among peasants and aristocrats. The activities of Rasputin can only be properly understood in the context of these settings.

Russia at the Turn of the Century

The vast multi-national empire was struggling to modernize: to continue the economic upsurge begun in the 1880s; to tackle peasant land-hunger by major reform; to enable popular participation in the political process by the introduction of a parliament, called the State Duma; and to raise public awareness by a huge expansion of the press and a reduction in state censorship.

In every area of state and public activity, the

tension between past practice and new initiative gave rise to conflicting political programmes. The central question was: how should Russia be governed? On becoming tsar Nicholas II swore to uphold the legacy of his father, Alexander III, who had been a committed autocrat, and who had espoused economic reform expressly in order to strengthen the autocracy. The autocracy – that is, the traditional Russian form of monarchy – was widely supported by the aristocracy and large sections of the gentry. Many, however, also believed that a form of constitutional monarchy, or shared power, was the way ahead. The peasants were piously loyal to the person of the tsar, but also longed for land reform that would give them greater autonomy and less control by the state, of which the tsar was the executive head.

The mentality of the fast-growing working class – mostly ex-peasants and poor town dwellers – was changing rapidly under the impact of harsh industrial working conditions and socialist propaganda, and it was becoming republican, if not outright revolutionary.

Standing outside this structure were the intelligentsia. They included politicians and journalists, writers and poets, composers and musicians, artists and critics, teachers, doctors and lawyers, scientists and engineers. Their ideas varied widely, but they shared a critical attitude towards the state and its effects on social development. Part of the intelligentsia plotted to overthrow the existing state, and the most extreme of them were organized by Vladimir Lenin into a party of 'professional revolutionaries', known as the Bolsheviks.

Nicholas ascended the throne in 1894, the year of his marriage to Princess Alix of Hesse-Darmstadt, a granddaughter of Queen Victoria, German by title but English by upbringing. On becoming a Romanov, Alix adopted Orthodox Christianity and changed her name to Alexandra, adopting the patronymic Fedorovna required of Russian empresses.

Nicholas's father, Alexander III, had ruled since 1881, applying economic policies designed to stimulate industry, business and commerce, and with dramatic success. By the end of the century Russia had been transformed into a major player in the world league of oil, steel, coal and wheat producers. But economic success brought with it industrial unrest, the organization of workers in illegal trade unions and their political agitation by Marxist revolutionaries. Equally, the export of grain had been achieved at the cost of depressed peasant consumption and low domestic prices. Workers and peasants reached a climax of discontent, with strikes and peasant revolts sweeping large areas of the country in the first years of the century.

Russia's small student population had been the seedbed of revolution since the middle of the nineteenth century, and in 1902 it, too, erupted in demonstrations, calling for intellectual freedom and democratic liberties. The unrest culminated in January 1905. A procession of 100,000 workers and their families, led by a priest and bearing icons and portraits of the tsar, marched towards the Winter Palace in St Petersburg with demands for economic and political improvements. The troops fired warning shots, and then opened fire on the crowd. Several hundred were killed and injured, and Nicholas II was cursed as Nicholas the Bloody.

Terrorism mounted, claiming senior government figures, including a close relative of the tsar. The turmoil peaked in October with a general strike that affected every aspect of public activity. Russia was challenging the tsar to compromise and allow society a voice in government.

The task facing Nicholas was enormous. Unprepared and untrained for his role as emperor, he lived with the memory of a father who had despised him. A muscular bully of a man, who lifted weights for exercise and played the trombone for cultural diversion, Alexander had dismissed Nicholas as a weak and indecisive failure, and Nicholas had accepted his father's judgement of him. He detested his state responsibilities and was happiest in the bosom of his adoring family, a country squire by nature with no stomach for confrontation with 'historic forces'.

The events of 1905 were complicated by war with Japan for possession of Manchuria. The Trans-Siberian Railway from European Russia to the Pacific was not complete when hundreds of thousands of troops had to be transported 10,000 kilometres to fight an unknown enemy, who had only to cross 300 kilometres of sea to put his forces on the mainland. While the civilian population was in revolt, the army was fighting – and mostly losing – battles in the Far East.

Virtually the entire Russian fleet was sunk by the Japanese in the Tsushima Straits on a single afternoon in May. In August 1905 the United States brokered a peace treaty that was less punitive for Russia than anticipated.

The tsar had sanctioned the war in the misguided belief that the empire's economic interests in the Far East could be secured by an easy victory over the forces of an 'inferior' Asiatic country. Now, faced by universal unrest at home and humiliation abroad, he was compelled at the end of October 1905 to succumb to the popular demand for representation. He issued a manifesto promising civil rights, including freedom of speech, conscience, assembly and association, and inviolability of the person; a broad franchise for elections to a national assembly (the State Duma); and representative government.

This surrender came to be known as the 1905 Revolution. But, as Leon Trotsky told a huge crowd at St Petersburg University, holding a copy of the manifesto aloft: 'The Tsar's Manifesto is nothing but a piece of paper. Today they give it to you, tomorrow they will tear it into bits, as I do now!'[1] And indeed, after violently suppressing the revolt, and with the state's coffers replenished by a huge foreign loan, the tsar watered down the concessions. The Duma was not elected by universal suffrage, but by an electoral system weighted in favour of (supposed) conservative forces. By the time the Duma convened in May 1906, it was clear that the tsar had no intention of allowing it to encroach on his God-given right to rule the empire as he saw fit. Confrontation and worsening relations between the monarch and his subjects was to be the order of the day.

The Romanov Tragedy

In the midst of internal and international strife, Nicholas II and his wife were facing yet another crisis, but it was one they dared not make public, fearing the damage it could do to the dynasty. They decided instead to keep it within the confines of their private family life.

By 1900 the empress had had three daughters in succession, and both she and her husband wanted a son to continue the Romanov dynasty. During a trip to France in 1901, the tsar's sister-in-law, Grand Duchess Militsa, persuaded the royal couple to consult a faith healer, Philippe Nizier-Vachod, who was reputed to be able to determine the sex of an unborn child. He was taken back to Russia with Nicholas and Alexandra, but the next child, her fourth, was also a girl, and when Vachod told the empress in 1903 that she was pregnant and she turned out not to be, he was sent packing. The next year, however, she did indeed give birth to a son, Alexei, the tsarevich or crown prince.

Romanov delight was dashed when it was found that Alexei was a haemophiliac. Like other descendants of Queen Victoria, Alexandra had already lost four male relatives, including a brother, to this blood disease. In haemophilia, prolonged bleeding occurs if the sufferer experiences even slight physical injury. Lacking the clotting agent without which the bleeding cannot stop spontaneously, the haemophiliac of ninety years ago, before the advent of blood transfusion and additives, had little choice but to endure the pain of the swelling, to lie quietly and wait, either for the gradual recovery of the blood vessels, which could take many weeks, or death itself.

The distraught parents of the tsarevich searched everywhere for a cure or at least some palliative treatment, but in vain. Medical science of the time could offer no comfort, still less a solution. They were therefore open to suggestions of alternative medicine, whether homeopathic, herbalist or spiritual. It was into this scene of family distress, overshadowed by national turmoil and political uncertainty, that a peasant from Siberia was introduced, in the hope that he possessed some magic power that would save Alexei's life.

The Formation of a Holy Man

Most of what is known about Rasputin has been the subject of mythology and is open to correction. He has often been called a mad monk, but he was neither mad nor a monk. Thought to have been born in 1872, in fact he was born on 10 January 1869. Said to have been nicknamed Rasputin because the Russian word *rasputnik* suited his reputation as a libertine, in fact his name was that of his forebears, who took their name from the word *rasputie*, which simply means a fork in the highway.

Gregory Rasputin was born in the village of Pokrovskoe, in the province of Tobolsk in Western Siberia. His father, Yefim, was a poor peasant who eked out a living on his smallholding, supplemented by a small carrier business. As a boy, Gregory helped his father in the fields and then gradually took over the transport trade. He was described as a well-built child who soon became the most daring of a gang of toughs. The priest of Pokrovskoe used to give him ten kopeks a week to stay away from church on Sundays. He became a well-known horse-thief and drunken hooligan, a wild boy with no respect for people or property, foul-mouthed and violent, and sexually precocious.

His confidence in handling women, which in Siberian culture was akin to a man's skill in mastering a horse, was perhaps one of the most reliable facts in his biography. Women of all classes responded to his domineering manner, submitting to his crude advances in sufficient number to gratify his reputedly gargantuan appetite. In due course, however, Rasputin's sexual powers were augmented by power of a different sort, and one that explains why his lustful exploits succeeded with such a wide variety of women, from peasant girls to the womenfolk of the highest in the land.

The young Gregory was not entirely given over to the life of a materialistic sensualist, however. The first indication that he might possess special qualities occurred when he was only a small boy. He was lying sick in bed when the villagers gathered in his father's house to discuss what to do about the theft of one of their horses, no small matter amid such poverty. The young Gregory suddenly sat up in bed and pointed to a man at the back of the room, declaring that he was the thief. As this turned out to be true, Gregory was assumed to possess second sight. In due course this became the gift of prophecy, demonstrated by his being able to predict the arrival of new faces in the village and, much later, of events of greater importance.

He was fascinated by religion, less in its ritualistic form – as the local priest's attitude showed – than in the idea of finding communion with God, in seeking the meaning of life through meditation, fasting and prayer. In effect, he was attracted to the life of a monk. He had heard a great deal about a monastery at Verkhoturye, in the neighbouring province of Perm, much of it from wandering 'holy men' who called at his father's house.

One account has it that when he was fourteen, after nearly killing an old man he had robbed, he was given twenty strokes of the whip in public, and the event aroused in him a fit of mysticism. He began frequenting churches and monasteries with an assiduity bordering on fanaticism. He would be seen at the roadside, praying incomprehensibly and lashing himself with thistles. People thought he was inspired, and roubles began pouring into the ever-present begging bowl. At about this time, he starting visiting Verkhoturye, always travelling on foot and staying for a month or two. Uneducated and illiterate, yet radiating a passion for spiritual knowledge, he intrigued the monks, and they would willingly engage him in long and searching discussion about God's ways.

When he returned to Pokrovskoe after his first retreat he was unrecognizable. He had given up tobacco and vodka, and now spoke in a disjointed way, nervously stroking his new beard, as he struggled to impart oracular significance to his mutterings. To some he was an absurd figure, the wild and disreputable Grishka (diminutive of Gregory) playing at being a man of God. But he found a ready and willing audience in his fellow peasants, who would sit by as he talked to them about religion and led them in singing hymns and psalms.

At the age of nineteen Rasputin met Praskovia Dubrovina, a peasant from a neighbouring village. Blonde with black eyes, homely rather than pretty, Praskovia was not 'easy', like his other conquests, and he had to wait six months before she would consent to marry him in 1888 or 1889. Practical and level-headed, she was the most stable element in Rasputin's turbulent life. She provided him with two daughters and two sons – their first-born son died aged six months – and until his death in 1916 she continued to provide a family home, never complaining about his prodigious womanizing. She would say that he had plenty to go round.

At about this time, 1890, while working in the fields, Rasputin claimed to have seen a vision of the Virgin Mary, and that she seemed to be telling him something. He immediately set off with his faithful follower, an ex-policeman called Pecherkin, to ask his mentor at Verkhoturye for guidance. His mentor was the hermit, Makary. A holy man known widely in Russia as a seer and healer, Makary had even visited the tsar and tsarina at Tsarskoe Selo. He now told Gregory that his vision meant he had been chosen by God for a great purpose, and that he must strengthen his spiritual power at the monastery on Mount Athos in Greece.

Rasputin and Pecherkin walked all the way to Mount Athos and were admitted as novices. They were also introduced to the homosexual practices of the brotherhood, which Rasputin apparently found deeply offensive. Leaving the monastery to make a pilgrimage to the Holy Land, Rasputin cursed Mount Athos as full of moral filth and vermin. Pecherkin, who had already taken the vows, remained behind.

After two years away, Gregory returned home, stopping on the way to consult Makary about Mount Athos. His teacher explained that evil was to be found everywhere and that the temptations were often strongest in the cloister, where renunciation should be final. He concluded that monastic life was not for Gregory, who must try to save his soul in the outside world.

Now committed to a spiritual path, however idiosyncratic, Rasputin became an ascetic, praying all day and forsaking meat. Again, he gathered the villagers and told them colourful stories about the sights he had seen on his pilgrimage to Jerusalem. He had acquired the status of a *strannik*, or wanderer, one who travelled on an unending journey of expiation, self-discovery and truth, perfecting his saintly tendencies, finding food and shelter in monasteries and hospices. Stranniks were a common feature of the Russian countryside, wandering the face of the land, preaching and teaching, often until they died. Rasputin continued until a particular moment in his life, when he stopped his wandering and was launched on his historic career.

RELIGION AND HIGH SOCIETY

Religious Trends

Since the late Middle Ages, sectarian groups had been a widespread feature of spiritual life in Russia, and especially so in Siberia, where remote villages were isolated from organized religion. Harassed by the state and condemned as heretics by the Church, sectarians embraced a spectrum of groups as broad as can be found in the West today.

In a multi-national and multi-cultural empire, such as Russia, the range of religious affiliation and belief was almost literally universal in its scope, from Lutheranism and Roman Catholicism, to the Armenian and Georgian forms of Orthodoxy, to Judaism, Islam, Buddhism, Confucianism, Shamanism. Every ethnic Russian, however, of whatever social class, was born a member of the

Orthodox Church, and intermarriage between an Orthodox and any other believer was permitted only if the 'outsider' converted to Orthodoxy.

The Orthodox liturgy was in Old Church Slavonic, and therefore all but incomprehensible to the unschooled. The priests in their gorgeous robes, the incense and the choral singing, the highly decorated buildings themselves, were all designed to create an aura of heavenly otherness. The congregation took no part in the service, except to cross themselves, to beat their foreheads on the floor, and to murmur 'Amen'.

The Russian peasants were the Church's most devoted followers and from it they derived spiritual peace and purification. But in the more remote parts of the empire, like Siberia, where serfdom had been unknown and where settlement had been brought about very often by escaped serfs from European Russia, or released convicts or other sorts of runaway, the prevailing 'ideology' of free living and free thinking provided the perfect soil for sectarian ideas to take root. This was what troubled the state about the sects: the demand to worship as one wished was close to the demand to govern oneself as one wished.

Because sexual activity occupied such a central place in Rasputin's 'religious practice', it was thought he belonged to the *Khlysty* sect. The word *khlyst* may be a corruption of the word Khrist, i.e. Christ, for the khlysts believed that many 'christs' could be born, through normal intercourse, rather than virgin birth. More significantly, they also believed that sin, especially through sex, could bring the sinner closer to God.

Less controversially, the word khlyst also means a whip. The khlysts were known to practise flagellation, to engage in ecstatic dancing and singing, climaxing in indiscriminate sexual contact. That is, they held orgies, where exhaustion was a means to purge body and soul. From this group form of engagement it was a simple step to the more focused form of 'purification' to be had from one-to-one intercourse.

One of Rasputin's many conquests would later record in her diary that, as they journeyed together by train to his village in Siberia, he 'tested' her repeatedly, doing to her what a husband alone is permitted to do. She concluded that she must be most impure, since he found it necessary to subject her to perpetual testing. The more the sin, the more the redemption. Rasputin may well have been a flagellant. He never lost his love of dancing himself into a state of exhaustion, even if it was to the strains of the gypsy violin and guitar in the nightclubs he would frequent in the capital later on.

Rasputin the Healer

When Rasputin was introduced into the small circle of the Imperial family, it was not as a holy man, but as a healer. Indeed, he never called himself a holy man: 'There is no holy man on earth,' he said. 'So long as man lives, he sins.'[1] By 1906 he had a reputation for being able to bring relief and even cures where trained physicians had failed. All peasant communities used various forms of native medicine, herbal or otherwise. Rasputin never prescribed medicine as such; not that he found these methods unacceptable.

It was a 'native' skill of a different kind that made him effective as a healer. He had an observed ability for inducing a state of calm and relaxation in his 'patients'. As a youth he had shown extraordinary skill in handling animals. Indeed, it had made him a highly successful horse-thief. He had the gift of being able to remove fear and tension, much as a hypnotist induces their suspension. He had shown the same calming and confidence-inducing qualities in his relations with children, whether sick or healthy. Everyone who recalled meeting Rasputin has referred to his eyes, commonly described as 'hypnotic'.

The French ambassador during the First World War, Maurice Paléologue, was a natural enemy of Rasputin, whom he suspected of urging the tsar to leave the war, and hence to abandon France and the Allies. He also felt typical intellectual disdain for Rasputin's alleged magical powers. Yet the impressions he recorded of his one and only meeting with Rasputin show that he, too, felt that there was something special in the eyes of the Siberian peasant.

He wrote in his diary: 'That afternoon, as I was visiting Madame O . . . the door of the drawing room suddenly opened with a crash. A tall man in a long, black caftan and heavy boots strode towards Madame O and gave her a smacking kiss. It was Rasputin. He shot a glance at me and asked, "Who is it?" Madame O told him. He replied: "Ah, the French ambassador! I'm glad to meet him. I have something to say to him, as a matter of fact." He began to talk so volubly that Madame O had no time to translate. This gave me the chance to examine him at my leisure. Brown hair, long and badly-combed; stiff, black beard; high forehead; large, jutting nose; powerful mouth. But the whole expression of the face was concentrated in his eyes – flax-blue, with a strange brilliance, depth and fascination. His gaze was at once piercing and caressing, ingenuous and astute, direct and remote. When his speech became animated, his pupils seemed to be charged with magnetism.'[2]

The doctor who treated Rasputin as a child for smallpox recalled that he had such an ardent expression in his eyes that even he felt strangely affected by it. He was affected of course by the reputation Rasputin had gained since those far-off days, but it is worth noting none the less that the doctor, too, remembered his eyes as of special significance.

Aron Simanovich, who became his personal secretary, recalled that he was struck by Rasputin's eyes, which 'riveted one and at the same time made one feel uncomfortable.'[3] His voice was also an important part of his persona: deep, soft, soothing and reassuring – very much a voice associated with the stock-in-trade of the hypnotist.

Rasputin himself denied that he practised hypnotism. He apparently associated it with spiritualism, which he allegedly abominated. Yet it was undeniably his eyes that played a part in his evident abilities as a healer. His daughter noted that nervous and impressionable people feel uneasy when clear blue eyes are fixed on them. She added that if the brilliance of the look is enhanced by the fervency of prayer, a veritable magnetic force is produced. She concluded that this was the basis of the almost miraculous cures obtained in some nervous diseases. And this was the basis of Rasputin's astounding career, once he had been introduced to the tsarevich in 1906.

Ironically, modern medicine is less sceptical than were Rasputin's contemporaries. The effect of calming on the blood vessels is well established. Soothing words, gentle music or restful pictures can be seen to reduce tension and blood pressure and hence to relax the blood vessels. Where the contraction of the blood vessels has caused the blood to accumulate at the site of a trauma – such as a haemophiliac experiences from even a minor bump – the effect of the relaxation is to allow the blood to disperse normally. Indian yogis routinely alter their bodily states by mental control. The connection between the mind where it affects mood, and the body where blood-flow is concerned, is no longer a matter of argument. It is therefore easier now than it was in Rasputin's day to accept, as a scientific certainty rather than as a mysterious 'magnetic force', that his skills as a healer were not a confidence trick, and especially that he was capable of doing good where the best medical practice had proved useless.

Rasputin and High Society

While on pilgrimage in Kazan in 1903, Rasputin was given a letter of introduction to Archimandrite Theofanes, who was spiritual adviser to the tsar. In St Petersburg, Rasputin stayed with Theofanes who in turn introduced him to the monk Father Iliodor, who was to play a fateful part in Rasputin's life. Having thus been given a taste of the highest level of the church hierarchy, and also a glimpse of its connection with high society, Rasputin returned home to Siberia.

In Kiev in 1905, he was introduced to Grand Duchess Anastasia, the wife of the tsar's cousin, Grand Duke Nikolai Nikolayevich, and her sister Militsa, who was married to his brother, Grand Duke Peter Nikolayevich. The two sisters wrote home to say that they had met a miraculous holy man and were urging him to come to St Petersburg. Fantastic tales had already been circulating about Rasputin, and the sisters believed that at last they had found the answer to the Empress's prayers. If Rasputin did not prove to be a healer for the tsarevich, surely no one would.

St Petersburg in the early years of the twentieth century was a hotbed of religious mania, coexisting with a climate of experimentation in art and philosophy, revolutionary politics, and new schools of medical and pseudo-medical science. All this was taking place against a background of profound social malaise, as it seemed the foundations of the regime were crumbling. Many people – intellectuals and others – were turning to religion, believing that the materialist doctrines of the nineteenth century had failed in 1905, and that self-perfection, rather than social perfection, was the surer path to salvation.

For unaccountable reasons, the women of Russian high society, however Orthodox, seemed prone to seeking religious ideas that excited rather than soothed their yearnings. Certainly among them were many highly impressionable ladies who found their excitement in the various new schools of mysticism that flourished. Spiritualism had become popular, with its table-tipping and glass-spinning and mystifying mediums who would bring messages from those who had 'passed over'. Charlatans and re-vamped music-hall acts were having a field-day. Healers were very much part of this scene. Hands were 'laid on', spells uttered, cards and tea-leaves read to find the appropriate treatment. It was a world made for someone like Rasputin, healer and holy man.

He arrived in St Petersburg on foot and went again to Theofanes. Soon, the Grand Duchesses Militsa and Anastasia were contacted by the tsarina's confidante, Anna Vyrubova, who said it was time to bring Rasputin to meet the tsar and tsarina. Anna Vyrubova was the daughter of the tsar's former head of chancery, and had been married off at the age of seventeen to a drunken and perverted naval officer. She had been scandalized by his behaviour on the first night and petitioned the tsar for a divorce, which he granted. Thereafter, her life consisted of supporting the empress in all her needs and endeavours. Before her marriage, she had met Rasputin and asked him to tell her if her marriage would be a success. He is said to have replied that it would be neither long nor a success. Having been proved right in his prediction, he was henceforth Anna's touchstone.

Stout and vulgar in appearance, and known at Court as 'the cook', Vyrubova supplied the empress with the kind of servility and discretion she felt she needed in the face of the hostility of her husband's relations. The dowager empress, in particular, was seen as the source of all of Alexandra's misfortunes. Certainly it was an odd friendship: one woman aristocratic and haughty, the other vulgar and garrulous. But since Alexandra was hostile to the establishment, she favoured those who were out of favour with society. She protected Vyrubova as she would later protect others regarded by the establishment as a menace to Russia's interests. Meanwhile, Anna was as indispensable to the empress as Rasputin was later to become.

Rasputin as Saviour

Having failed to find help for her son among the best doctors, the empress turned to God. To deserve His intervention, however, she must be even more pious and pure than she felt by nature. Disdainful of Court life in the capital, and fearful of the tsar's relatives whom she suspected of wanting to depose him as an inadequate autocrat, she drew her family into a small, self-sufficient circle outside St Petersburg at Tsarskoe Selo.

Every time the tsarevich recovered from one of his bouts, the tsarina felt that God had heard her prayers. And every time the inevitable accident occurred, she was plunged again into despair. It was when she was at her lowest ebb that Rasputin entered the scene and told her: 'Believe in the power of my prayers; believe in my help and your son will live.' Eager to believe in something, she believed in him. She felt that this lowly peasant had been sent by God to save her son, who was Russia's future hope. She persuaded herself that her son's life was in Rasputin's hands.

For her, Rasputin was more than a wanderer who performed miracles. He was a *starets*, a kind of guru, an ascetic who usually lived in a monastery, often as a hermit, a guide of souls to whom the troubled could turn in need. Often the starets was a former wandering pilgrim who had settled in one place. Once an individual has selected his starets, he gives him his soul in complete submission. The starets in turn is guided by God to find the best way to bring his disciple peace of mind. A number of startsy – plural of starets – rose to great heights of public esteem and became Orthodox saints. Their influence as unofficial clergy was considerable, far greater in the provinces than that of the priests.

The empress's conversion from her native Lutheranism to Russian Orthodoxy on her marriage to Nicholas had been a genuine act of faith. Orthodoxy, which promoted ritual and mysticism, rather than theology, suited her personality, and her imagination was fired by its archaism and simplicity. In her eyes, Rasputin acquired all the prestige and sanctity of a starets. As a peasant, he represented the 'true Russia', close to God and knowing the meaning of life. Because they were bound to the soil by its seasonal demands, peasants were often seen as living in an organic harmony with Nature, and they therefore found no difficulty in believing in God and feeling His presence.

Siberia too represented a Russia still unadulterated by Western habits, by cities and factories, a pure and simple Russia where an unspoiled peasantry supposedly held the secret of the moral life, and would one day save the rest of Russia from its present state of decay. Rasputin seemed to be everything the royal couple could wish for.

The doctors had said the tsarevich's death from haemophilia was inevitable. The boy would suffer periodic attacks of haemorrhaging and eventually one would prove fatal. During a particularly serious attack, with the doctors impotent, the empress had sought a spiritual healer for her son. Anna Vyrubova had told her of Rasputin's powers, and in November 1906 the former horse-thief from Pokrovskoe had boarded the train for Tsarskoe Selo fifteen miles from the capital, where the empress was waiting expectantly.

News of Alexei's illness came as a surprise to Rasputin. The isolation of the imperial family ensured that the seriousness of the case was kept secret. He was taken to the tsarevich's bedroom in the Alexander Palace, where he knelt and prayed.

He laid his hand on the boy's affected leg and said: 'There's a good boy, you'll be all right, but only God can tell what will happen tomorrow.' Almost at once the tsarevich began to recover.

THREE

GROWING FAME

Fame and Notoriety

Rasputin had already established his reputation as a healer and mystical fortune-teller in the capital. Indeed, his reputation had preceded him, partly because of the publicity provided by the two grand duchesses, but also by a rich widow called Lydia Bashmakova. Seeking solace in religion, Bashmakova found it in Rasputin. She taught him to read and did much to publicize his prowess. The press had carried reports of his miraculous healing: 'He is especially the providence of women, whom he purifies and consoles in the name of the Supreme Being. He visits the [public bath-houses] and brings the holy word to those who bathe . . . when they leave the baths they are not only physically but morally cleansed.'[1] The practice of 'preaching at the baths' was to cause Rasputin problems in due course.

Rasputin's apartment, rented and furnished by Bashmakova, was always packed, especially once it became known that he was advising the royal family. In due course, the Interior Ministry created a large team of detectives to provide security, as well as to collect information on Rasputin's activities. They watched the street where he lived, and guarded the staircase to his rooms.

It was not difficult to extract detailed information from Rasputin's visitors as they left their audience with him, and the reports filed at the police department were detailed. They noted that people were waiting for two or three days to consult him, and that he tended to see only the young and pretty women, declaring that the others had fewer sins to expiate. There was no fixed price for consultations, but his secretary, Striapchev, who had been under police surveillance in Tobolsk, would demand at least 100 roubles, all the money apparently set aside to build a church at Pokrovskoe. Already an honoured guest at the mansions and fine apartments of the rich and powerful, Rasputin now acquired virtually superhuman status as a confidant of no less than the empress herself. No one was yet to know why he visited her: the secret of the tsarevich's affliction was still closely guarded, and it says something for Rasputin's discretion, despite his laxity in other areas, that he did not breach the confidence placed in him.

Spirituality for Rasputin did not mean abstention. On the contrary, those who preached redemption through sin must sin themselves. Indeed, he argued that the day pretty girls no longer found in him the ardent exorcist who cleansed them of their sins, no one would take him seriously. And St Petersburg proved to be an excellent proving ground. There were the bath-houses with their separate massage cubicles, nightclubs and expensive restaurants, where a female following that included gypsy dancers, prostitutes and society ladies, was in constant attendance.

When the tsar was informed of Rasputin's activities, and advised to break off the contact, he assured his police informant that he knew that Rasputin preached the scriptures in the bath-houses. When such reports were submitted to the tsarina, she refused point blank to believe them. She simply could not imagine her friend behaving in this way. The tsar was less fanatical in his dedication and several times suggested that Rasputin should go home to Siberia for a break. On such occasions, Rasputin would board the Trans-Siberian express, taking with him anything up to a dozen female friends as company on the long journey, and as acolytes eager to learn the simple ways of the Russian peasants in their natural habitat.

His financial adviser, Aron Simanovich — a jeweller to the rich, including the royal family — recalled that Rasputin's female admirers were of two types: those who believed in his supernatural powers, his holiness and his divine calling, and those who simply thought it fashionable to be seen with him, or wanted to gain some advantage for themselves or their relatives through knowing him. 'When he was reproached for his weakness for women, he usually said it was not all his fault, as very many highly placed personages would simply throw their mistresses and even their wives at him in order to gain something for themselves, and most of the women who were intimate with him did so with their lovers' or husbands' consent.'[2]

Rasputin's power extended far beyond his attraction for women. He created a network of influence which grew and developed in power to such an extent that after the revolution of March 1917, the Provisional Government established a commission to investigate the causes of the collapse, and one of its chief concerns was to measure Rasputin's influence. According to secret police reports, Rasputin received huge commissions from businessmen he had introduced, and on the tsar's orders the Interior Ministry was paying out 5,000 roubles a month towards the end, and even that was not enough.

It seems that Rasputin never asked for money from his rich supporters, and could have been wealthy had he wished. His bills were paid by others, whether for rent, clothes or carousing, and he asked for money only when it was for someone else, especially if it was for a peasant. If a rich man and a poor person arrived at his apartment together, he would ask the rich man to give a few hundred roubles straight away. He sometimes sent petitioners to millionaires with a note asking for a favour. Senior government officials became accustomed to Rasputin's 'little notes', which in due course it was inadvisable to ignore.

Meanwhile, he did not allow his popularity to change his habits. On the contrary, he remained the coarse muzhik who would never tug a forelock to the nobility or show the least regard for the hierarchy. He made no attempt to acquire the manners of society, but behaved in aristocratic salons like a complete boor, perhaps on purpose. Princesses, famous actors and powerful ministers all toadied to him, although he behaved towards them with complete disregard for their elevated status. Peasants were treated by him gently, but the aristocracy and nobility were greeted with disdain. For no other reason than perverse pleasure, he could curse a high-born lady in gutter language, and the presence of a husband or father made no difference.

Yet few ever complained. Women would kiss his food-stained fingers, oblivious of his dirty fingernails. They would receive bits of food that he would share out among them with his hands, and think it a blessing. One of his favourite dishes was fish soup, in which he would soak lumps of black bread, then scoop them out and hand them around to his guests who would lap them up.

Few could watch him eat without a feeling of disgust. He rarely used a knife and fork, preferring his long, bony fingers, tearing the food apart like an animal. He had a large mouth in which only blackened stumps were visible as teeth. He ate no meat, sweets or pastries, preferring potatoes and vegetables above all. He had given up vodka before leaving Siberia, but in the monasteries he had acquired a taste for Madeira. When he went out drinking, he was accompanied by a police car carrying twenty bottles of Madeira.

In 1910, while visiting his long-suffering wife and family in Pokrovskoe, Rasputin suggested they return with him to live in the capital, where the girls and his son could attend school. Praskovia refused, as she hated the very idea of big cities, but she allowed Gregory to take the two girls, Maria and Varvara, with him. The family servant, Katya, went with them, but Dmitri, who may have been retarded, remained at home.

Understandably, Rasputin's daughter, Maria, recalled her father in a more favourable light than that cast on him by virtually all of the record. Yet much of her testimony rings both true and characteristic. For instance, she claims that Rasputin was a strict father, that he never allowed his daughters to go out alone, rarely permitted them to go to a matinée, and that later on, when young men began to show an interest in them, he proved the strictest of mentors. 'None of them,' she claims, 'had a right to more than half an hour's tête-à-tête; after that had elapsed, my father burst into the room and showed the poor lad the door. Prayers were given more than half an hour – morning and night.'[3]

Similarly, it was not the drunken, lecherous night-owl that Maria knew, but a typical Russian peasant, always simple and courteous in his manners, and treating everyone the same way. A samovar was always steaming on the table and visitors, whether noble or lowly, would be offered the same plain food as the family ate: potatoes, pickled cabbage and black bread, though it was also common for guests to bring caviar, fine fish and fruit to enrich the spread. He was overjoyed when a peasant brought cakes or chickens, and he would give in return money, an icon or whatever a rich visitor had left for him.

Maria denies that her father ever received money from the tsar or his wife, and claims that at the time of his death there were only 3,000 roubles in his bank account. Other money, kept in his desk, was missing. The fact that Rasputin received a pension on the tsar's instruction does not contradict Maria's point, of course, since the money came ostensibly from the state and not the tsar's own pocket. Maria also argues that the rumours of Rasputin's great wealth arose because unscrupulous hangers-on demanded huge sums from the gullible rich as the price of an introduction, sometimes as much as 10,000 roubles, while a would-be minister, hoping that Rasputin would use his influence with the tsar, might pay 50,000 roubles to the contact man. None of this money, Maria insisted, went to her father, but merely served to create an aura of corrupt wealth in his name.

Be that as it may, the fact is that Rasputin could not only afford to live in the centre of the capital, in an apartment big enough to accommodate a large number of daily petitioners; to support a wife and three children, in Pokrovskoe and St Petersburg; to make the long journey home fairly often; to rebuild his house in the village, making it the biggest one there, but also to finance the construction of a church and a hospital.

Rasputin's Circle

Rasputin's politics were also not straightforward. As an ignorant peasant with a deep devotion to the tsar and the autocracy, we would expect him to favour the extremist right-wing politics of the anti-Semitic parties that arose in the aftermath of the 1905 revolution. Apart from their contempt for liberalism, their bitterest complaint was that Nicholas II had gone cap in hand to Jewish bankers in Paris in order to refill the treasury's coffers after the Russo-Japanese War. Not only had Russia been humiliated by an inferior Asiatic nation – as they saw it – but she had also sold herself to the most hated of all Jewish symbols, the banks.

As for Rasputin, the right-wing Union of Russian People had hoped that he would uphold their position at Court and do his best to ensure that the tsar made no further concessions. However, although he generally favoured them because they supported the autocracy, which he cherished, he was no one's puppet. He spoke his mind and toed no party line. He argued that rebellions and political opposition stemmed from those who kept the people in ignorance, deprived them of hospitals and schools and gave them nothing but vodka to drown their sorrows. 'Instead of organizing pogroms and blaming the Jews for every evil,' he said, 'we would do better to criticize ourselves.'[4]

This was not the kind of sentiment the proto-fascists of the Union of Russian People wanted to hear from their supposed agent. Nor could they be pleased to know that he was also lending an ear to the special pleading of his adviser, Simanovich, whose influential friends in the Jewish community were pressing him to recruit Rasputin in the cause of Jewish equal rights. Simanovich knew as well as any that anti-Semitism was endemic in Russia, among the upper no less than among the lower classes, but he persuaded himself that it could have been eradicated without difficulty, had the will to do so existed. His was, however, a hopeless case. The only comfort the emperor could find, against the recent evidence of universal discontent, was to believe, as he told a French diplomat in 1909, that the peasants and gentry and army were all loyal, and that 'the revolutionary elements are composed above all of Jews, students, landless peasants and a few workers.'[5]

Politics in the capital was far from restricted to the Jewish Question, however. For the royal couple, Rasputin was expected to express the sentiments of all right-wing elements. The concerns of Simanovich and his friends were not to be voiced in such company.

The central question after the 1905 revolution was how far the tsar and his government would permit the new parliament, the State Duma, to go in its opposition to government legislation, and what issues the Duma chose on which to make its attacks most effective. With a vastly enlarged press which was able to report the Duma debates, and parliamentary immunity for deputies, the age of public political scandal and rumour came to Russia with a vengeance. The reputedly constant presence at Court of a notorious charlatan – which is how everyone but his disciples saw him – made Rasputin just such a target.

In late 1910 the governess of the young grand duchesses complained to the empress that Rasputin had been loitering in their quarters as they were preparing for bed, and she felt that this was potentially scandalous. The empress, instead of being mortified by the revelation, was furious at the woman's impudence. The tsar, however, was more realistic and persuaded Alexandra to forbid any further visitations by their 'Friend' to such a sensitive area of the palace. The governess, a Miss Tyutcheva, was dismissed. As a member of a distinguished Moscow family with royal connections, however, she made sure that everyone of influence knew what was going on in the bosom of the royal family.

By this time, there was a widespread belief that Rasputin had become the centre of an elaborate conspiracy or caucus that was pursuing its own political agenda. Sometimes called the Black Bloc or Rasputin Circle, in fact no such conspiracy existed. It was, however, certainly true that a large number of shady individuals prowled around Rasputin with the intention of penetrating the palace through Anna Vyrubova, the intimate friend of both Rasputin and the empress. Far from constituting a bloc, however, they intrigued against each other as they jockeyed for the best position to advance their own candidates. By engaging Rasputin's support, each faction or individual was at various times responsible for the replacement of a minister or high official by someone of their own choice.

The combination of rich, ambitious and influential patrons, police reports about scandalous public behaviour, and apparently easy access to the palace, made Rasputin into a potential time-bomb at the feet of the royal family. At the beginning of 1911 senior figures decided that the way to eliminate Rasputin was to expose him as a sectarian. The prime minister, Peter Stolypin, failed, however, to convince the tsar, who told him he should meet Rasputin himself. Stolypin told Mikhail Rodzianko, president of the Duma, what transpired when he met the starets:

Rasputin ran his pale eyes over me, mumbled mysterious and inarticulate words from the Scriptures, made strange movements with his hands, and I began to feel an indescribable loathing for this vermin sitting opposite me. Still, I did realize that the man possessed great hypnotic power, which was beginning to produce a fairly strong [emotional] impression on me, though certainly one of repulsion. I pulled myself together and, addressing him roughly, told him that on the strength of the evidence in my possession I could annihilate him by prosecuting him as a sectarian. I then ordered him to leave St Petersburg immediately of his own free will for his native village and never show his face here again.[6]

Accordingly in March 1911, Rasputin went on his second pilgrimage to Jerusalem, and then returned home to Pokrovskoe, where friends from the capital, including Father Iliodor, came to see him. During all this time, the empress and the royal family remained in touch with their mentor by writing letters that were delivered, via Vyrubova, by imperial courier. While staying at Rasputin's house in Pokrovskoe, Father Iliodor managed to steal some of these, one of which would serve as a highly compromising document.

Written by an empress to her religious instructor, this letter can be seen today for what it was: an expression of the sort of unctuous piety that was characteristic of her hysterical style. Seen by Rasputin's enemies, and by those who wished to weaken the bond of patronage he enjoyed at Court, however, it was a letter to Russia's most notorious sexual miscreant: 'My much loved never to be forgotten teacher, saviour and instructor,' Alexandra wrote. 'I am so wretched without you. My soul is only rested and at ease when you, my teacher, are near me. I kiss your hands and lay my head upon your blessed shoulders. I feel so joyful then. Then all I want is to sleep, sleep for ever on your shoulder, in your embrace. It is such happiness to feel your presence close to me. Where are you, where have you run off to? . . . Come back soon. I await you and yearn for you. I ask for your holy blessing and kiss your blessed hands. Your eternally loving Mama.'[7] He always referred to her as 'Mama' and to the tsar as 'Papa', and they to him as 'Our Friend'.

FOUR

TRIAL AND TRIBULATION

After a few months in Pokrovskoe, Rasputin returned, not to St Petersburg, but to Kiev, where that autumn the royal family arrived for the ceremonial inauguration of local self-government in south-western Russia. This institutional initiative had emerged from a conflict between Stolypin and the tsar. Both houses of the Duma had rejected it and it had been introduced by Stolypin as emergency legislation. He was thus compromised in the eyes of the tsar, and a campaign against him at Court was rumoured to have been orchestrated, according to Rodzianko, by the 'Rasputin faction'.

Rasputin had apparently warned the tsar against the Kiev visit, prophesying that Stolypin would be assassinated. On this occasion, Nicholas ignored the advice. Furthermore, the empress asked Vyrubova to ensure that 'Father Gregory' would also be in

Kiev, in case he was needed by the tsarevich. As predicted, in full view of the tsar in a Kiev theatre, Stolypin was assassinated by a police agent. Rasputin was quick to reassure the tsar that Stolypin had had nothing left to offer anyway, a view that was soon confirmed by Stolypin's autopsy, which showed he had only a few months to live. Rasputin's prophetic powers seemed undiminished.

By this time, Rasputin was plainly a factor in Russian politics, but his former supporters among the Church hierarchy had by now lost faith in their 'discovery'. His public debauchery and his claim to speak as a man of God were an affront that they wanted to eliminate. His influence at Court, moreover, eclipsed that of the Church dignitaries themselves, and personal sensibilities were offended.

In December 1911, Bishop Hermogenes and Father Iliodor decided to bring the errant starets to book. A tribunal was convened and Rasputin was summoned to hear the charges. His former friend, Iliodor, who had accompanied him on a tour of religious establishments, voiced his disgust at Rasputin's behaviour with women, and testified that Rasputin had tried to enter the cell of every nun in the convents they visited, adding that he had no intellectual or supernatural power, no sense of honour, and above all was coarse in his references to the royal family. In particular, he had begun to boast that he was intimate with the empress.

The tribunal, however, quickly descended into farce, as first a witness and then the bishop himself physically assaulted Rasputin, who managed to escape with his life by fleeing the place. He at once reported the incident to Vyrubova who in turn told the tsar and tsarina. As a result, Hermogenes, a highly popular figure among the most reactionary, if also the lower, classes, was exiled to a miserable provincial monastery, where he blamed himself for having launched Rasputin in the first place. He remained there until 1917, when he was murdered by the Bolsheviks. Iliodor was imprisoned for a short time in another monastery.

Rasputin was triumphant. He gave interviews to the press, creating an impression that he felt invincible, that his protection at Court was such that he could even cast as popular a figure as Hermogenes into oblivion. The impression was reinforced by a ban, imposed by the tsar, on any further mention of Rasputin's name in the newspapers. But the complaints kept mounting. For instance, the Holy Synod was informed by an elderly baroness that Rasputin had swindled her out of 270,000 roubles by posing as her late husband who had been dead for thirty years. He had held a seance in which Jesus, played by one of his accomplices, had appeared to the widow and ordered her to hand over all her money to Rasputin. Even the florist who supplied the crown of thorns was discovered.

The most damaging episode, however, occurred at the beginning of 1912, and it resulted from an almost suicidal act of revenge by Father Iliodor. During the previous summer Iliodor had accompanied Rasputin to his home in Pokrovskoe, and while there he had stolen letters from the tsar's daughters and the empress, including the one with the endearing contents cited above. Now he had this letter copied and circulated.

Rasputin was sufficiently shaken by the disclosures to call on the new prime minister, Kokovtsev, himself. The prime minister urged him to leave St Petersburg in order to limit the damage his behaviour was causing the tsar. It was advice that Rasputin felt it prudent to follow, and in mid-

January 1912 he went home to Siberia, where his disgrace provided much pleasure to the villagers, who felt that he had risen much too high above himself.

Meanwhile, the leader of one of the most powerful parties in the Duma, Alexander Guchkov, a rich industrialist who saw the situation at Court as an opportunity to undermine the autocracy and shift more power to parliament, planned to bring matters to a head by opening a debate on the Rasputin question. He raised the issue in the Duma, which was damaging enough, but Rodzianko managed to avert an escalation of this open confrontation with the tsar by offering to show Nicholas in private audience a dossier on Rasputin's activities, expecting that the tsar would at last see sense and break off relations with Rasputin for good.

While Nicholas was plainly affected, he told Rodzianko that the family depended on Rasputin to treat the tsarevich, and since it was purely a family matter, he could allow no outside interference. The tsar and tsarina already despised the Duma, as an institution designed to reduce the authority of the monarchy. Now, Guchkov and Rodzianko became figures of personal hatred who wanted to undermine the royal family itself by attacking its most dedicated and indispensable supporter. Rodzianko was by no means an opponent of either the tsar or the principle of monarchy, but he was among those who were convinced of the existence of a Rasputin-inspired conspiracy, and the tsar's defensive response to the damaging evidence about Rasputin did nothing to change his mind.

Rasputin was now recalled from Pokrovskoe, and in March 1912 was included by the empress in the royal party that left the capital in the imperial train for their annual journey to the Crimea. He left the train shortly after it left St Petersburg, as Nicholas thought it prudent for him to travel alone, which he duly did, only arriving at Yalta three days later. His arrival, which the royal couple intended to keep secret, was leaked and there were awkward exchanges with the local police and the minister of the interior, who was in Yalta to supervise security arrangements. As a result, Rasputin only remained there a short while before returning to Pokrovskoe where he remained until the autumn.

Meanwhile in September the royal family moved to their Polish summer residences, the hunting estates at Bialowieze and Spala. After an uneventful and healthy summer, disaster struck at Bialowieze, when the tsarevich hurt his knee while getting into his bath (some sources suggest it was while getting into a boat), with the usual consequences. He was well enough to accompany the family when it set off for Spala, but en route he became seriously ill and soon a large tumour formed in his groin, as the internal bleeding built up. He was in great pain. His doctors, summoned from St Petersburg, were helpless. For the first time it was decided that the public should be informed of the boy's condition, and bulletins were issued, including even a draft announcement of his death. The tsarevich was given the last sacraments and public prayers were ordered.

In a final act of desperation, on 12 October the empress asked Vyrubova to send a telegram to Rasputin in Siberia. He received it the next day and at once knelt in prayer before an icon. An hour later he sent a telegram saying: 'Fear nothing. The malady is not as dangerous as it seems to be. Do not let the doctors bother him too much.'[1] The telegram arrived at Spala on the 14th, and two days later Alexei was out of danger.

Rasputin in 1906

Rasputin with his sponsor, Bishop Hermogenes, and friend, Father Iliodor, in 1906

Nicholas and Alexandra in sixteenth-century Muscovite dress in 1913, the 300th anniversary of the Romanov dynasty

Felix Yusupov in sixteenth-century boyar costume for a ball at the Albert Hall, London, 1910

Anna Vyrubova, the empress's confidante and go-between

Cartoons depicting Rasputin's influence at Court, on the eve of the First World War

The empress at tea with Rasputin. Behind her stands her daughter, Anastasia. The child on the right does not appear to be the tsarevich

A gathering of admirers at Rasputin's apartment in 1915

Rasputin at Pokrovskoe with his children, Maria, Varvara and the retarded Dmitri, in 1910

The tsarevich and his father, both dressed in Guards uniform, at the time of the First World War

The tsar blesses troops at the front, 1915

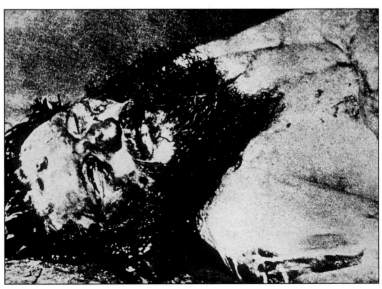

Police photo of Rasputin after discovery in the river, January 1917

Whether the telegram itself could have produced the same effect as the presence of its sender, or the advice to keep the doctors away was enough to reduce the stress and promote a recovery, or whether a spontaneous remission was about to occur, cannot be established with any greater authority than the belief that a miracle had occurred.

The empress needed no persuading that God had intervened and taken pity on her and her son, thanks only to the dedicated intercession of her loyal Friend, Father Gregory. Who now could possibly shake her trust in him, and how could her husband even dare to think of separating her from this bulwark of moral strength in her trying life?

FIVE

WAR AND SPY MANIA

War

An elaborate plot to assassinate Rasputin almost succeeded in June 1914 – on the very day Archduke Franz Ferdinand and his wife were shot in Sarajevo – while he was at home in Pokrovskoe. Father Iliodor had encouraged one of his more demented supporters, a prostitute and former lover of Rasputin's, called Chionya Guseva, to murder him. Disfigured by syphilis, Guseva disguised herself as a beggar and at an appropriate moment, in full public view, she managed to plunge a knife into Rasputin's abdomen. A doctor was called from Tiumen and after the eight-hour journey managed to operate. Rasputin refused anaesthetic and was patched up sufficiently to be taken back 58 miles by road to Tiumen for further treatment.

Meanwhile, the royal family had been informed, as well as the press. Nicholas ordered increased security and the tsarina sent a leading surgeon to tend her Friend. Professor von Breden reopened the wound and corrected dangerous mistakes. Guseva was arrested, declared insane and unfit for trial. Her family petitioned for her release, and the doctor in charge concluded that his patient was suffering from nothing more serious than 'psychic agitation and a heightened religious disposition,'[1] yet she was kept in custody and not released until March 1917. No doubt it was felt by the authorities that what she might say at a trial could embarrass the tsar and his wife.

While Rasputin was convalescing, the First World War broke out. A committed pacifist, he had written to the tsar a year earlier, urging him to do everything to preserve peace in the Balkans, where war fever was mounting. While arguing that Christians should not kill each other as a matter of principle, he showed himself to be no primitive pro-Slav by also pointing out that the Ottoman Turks had a better record of religious tolerance than the Orthodox, 'but it comes out different in the newspapers'. At the same time, Nicholas was being urged by Rodzianko that 'war will be accepted with joy and will serve only to increase the power and prestige of the imperial power,' and that Russia could profit from this by seizing the Straits from Turkey.[2]

Rasputin voiced his fear of war in telegrams to Nicholas II, warning that it would be disastrous for the royal family. But Nicholas was in no mood to forego the pleasure of the huge wave of support for the war and, as he believed, for the regime, and was therefore in no mood to appear weak in the face of German militarism. Nor was he well disposed towards Gregory at the time. Rasputin tried to penetrate the tsar's wall of silence by writing a letter in a tone of apocalyptic prophecy:

. . . A terrible storm cloud hangs over Russia. Disaster, grief, murky darkness and no light. A whole ocean of tears . . . and so much blood. What can I say? I can find no words to describe the horror. I know they all want you to go to war, the most loyal, and they do not know that they [are bringing] destruction. Heavy is God's punishment; when he takes away men's understanding it is the beginning of the end. You are the tsar, the father of your people, don't let the lunatics triumph and destroy you and

the people, and if we conquer Germany, what in
truth will happen to Russia? . . . We all drown in
blood. The disaster is great, the misery infinite.[3]

The empress was equally desperate that Russia
should not enter the war, though, like Gregory, she
felt that once war was declared Russia must make
the supreme effort to ensure victory. She set about
organizing military hospitals and, with her two
elder daughters and Anna Vyrubova, quickly
acquired sufficient nursing skills to take on a wide
variety of caring tasks in the hospital she set up at
Tsarskoe Selo.

Some time during the summer, probably when he
knew his life had been saved after Guseva's attempt,
Rasputin asked the tsar's permission to add the
suffix Novy, i.e. New, to his name. This has
sometimes been mistaken for his real name, with
Rasputin as the 'scandalous' sobriquet. In fact,
Rasputin was his real name and Novy simply
suggests the new man emerged from mortal danger.

With the tsarevich in good health and so much
work to do, Alexandra had little time to spare for
her spiritual mentor when he returned to the
capital in September 1914, and he was not best

pleased. Moreover, although the empress and Anna Vyrubova were now working together, much of the intimacy had gone out of their friendship, as Alexandra had begun to feel jealous of Anna's growing closeness to the tsar since the beginning of the year. This, too, meant that the tsarina was not as accessible to Rasputin as she had been.

In January 1915, however, Rasputin's fortunes revived once again. Anna Vyrubova was seriously injured in a train crash and not expected to live. At the crucial moment, with the royal couple and her family at her bedside, Rasputin entered the room unexpectedly, uttered some soothing words, prophesied that she would not die, and left. Anna at once began to recover and was soon back at work, though lame as Rasputin had predicted. The tsar's faith in Rasputin's healing powers was restored, while that of the empress and Anna, which had never failed, soared.

Rasputin's position was as strong as it had ever been. The tsar had ordered reinforced security after the attempt on his life, and he was once again the centre of devotion among the same mostly female clientele. But the trauma in Pokrovskoe took its toll. His ability to focus his energy seems to have been weakened, and he made great efforts to restore it by long hours of prayer and meditation. His daughter claims that it was also only now that he began to drink seriously. Certainly the police reports indicate that drunken brawls and appalling behaviour were even more wild than they had been.

His scandalous behaviour reached its peak, not in Petrograd – as St Petersburg had been renamed in August 1914 to replace its Germanic sound with something suitably Slavonic – but in Moscow, in March 1915. He had gone there to pray to a particular icon, ostensibly to fulfil a promise to God at the time of the attempt on his life, but in practice to acquire publicity to help bolster his image. Having done his spiritual duty, he then repaired to a celebrated Moscow night spot, the Yar Restaurant, where, accompanied by two journalists and three young women, he took a private room with a gypsy band.

Stirred by his favourite rhythms, and fired by the drink and the female company, Gregory was soon his old self again, leering and groping, but above all boasting about his relations with the empress. Displaying his shirt, he said she had personally embroidered it. He could make her do anything, he bragged. 'Yes, I, Grishka Rasputin. I could make her dance like this if I wanted to,' he said with an obscene gesture.[4]

The general racket brought others into the room, and Rasputin must have been provoked, perhaps by someone voicing doubt that he really was Rasputin, into dropping his breeches and exposing himself, waving his penis as if to prove his identity. The shrieks of women and smashing of glass finally brought the police, but neither they nor the management dared to throw him out. It was only after the chief of police himself arrived that the miscreant was led away, only to be released next morning. He promptly departed for the capital, accompanied to the train by a party of women.

Rasputin's enemies were overjoyed at the news of the scandal. Surely his public disgrace of the empress would at long last bring the woman to her senses! The interior minister, Nikolai Maklakov, however, produced a watered-down report for the tsar, and it was not until several months later, in June 1915, when Maklakov was replaced by Prince Nikolai Shcherbatov, that Nicholas was fully informed. He summoned Rasputin and angrily demanded an explanation. The hapless muzhik gave the usual sob story of the innocent peasant out of his depth, and above all swore that the allegations about the empress were a lie. Nicholas was less than convinced, and ordered him to leave for Pokrovskoe, and an apparently chastened Rasputin departed at once.

The empress was visibly distressed when she was shown the report, but her reaction was not defensive, like that of her husband, but combative:

> If we let our Friend be persecuted we and our country shall suffer for it . . . I am so weary, such heartache and pain from all this – the idea of dirt being spread about one we venerate is more than horrible. Ah, my love, when *at last* will you thump with your hand upon the table and scream at Djunkovsky [the chief of police] and others when they act wrongly – one does not fear you – and one *must* – they must be frightened of you otherwise all sit upon us.[5]

The tsar sacked Djunkovsky in August 1915, but the new interior minister, Shcherbatov, was determined to eliminate what he and most other senior officials saw as the stark danger to the throne posed by Rasputin's presence. He relaxed press censorship enough to allow the publication of a number of articles accusing Rasputin of being pro-German. Couched in terms of self-criticism, one article observed that the establishment's toleration of such a tarnished figure as Rasputin was 'the most conclusive condemnation of a regime whose treachery and vacillations have become common gossip . . . We are so accustomed to scandal that not even this scandal has disturbed us much.'[6] Shcherbatov was sacked after three months and replaced by Alexei Khvostov, whose relations with Rasputin were complex, nefarious and corrupt.

Rasputin had been told by his friend, Barnaby, whom he had helped become a bishop, that Khvostov, then governor of Nizhny Novgorod, had offered to try and make peace between Rasputin and Iliodor, and was hoping to be given the job of interior minister in recompense. When they met, Barnaby said to Rasputin: 'This is the fat man I cabled you about.'[7] Rasputin asked Khvostov what his relations with Iliodor were, and the would-be minister replied that Iliodor did whatever he told him to. 'What if I wanted him banished?' Rasputin asked. 'If Iliodor knows I'm against him,' Khvostov said, 'he'll evaporate of his own accord. You have nothing to fear from him.'[8]

Reassured, when he arrived in the capital, Rasputin asked the Tsar to make Khvostov interior minister and, since Shcherbatov was about to be dismissed, Nicholas obliged. In due course Khvostov starting putting pressure on Iliodor, who fled to Norway from where he continued his attacks on Rasputin.

In fact, the flight to Norway had been arranged by Khvostov himself, who had given Iliodor 60,000 roubles from a secret fund. Khvostov knew that Rasputin could have him removed as easily as he had had him appointed, and he therefore plotted with Iliodor to find a way to assassinate Rasputin. At this point, a third person entered the scene. Deputy Interior Minister Beletsky, who very much wanted to be minister, was intercepting Iliodor's correspondence, having suborned Khvostov's own agent, a journalist called Rzhevsky. Rzhevsky had received letters from Khvostov to take to Norway, as well as more money to organize the attempt, and now wanted to be introduced to Rasputin so that he could expose the plot.

When Rasputin was shown Khvostov's letter he

was furious. A meeting took place at Vyrubova's, at which Simanovich showed Khvostov's letter to the empress. Belyaev, the deputy war minister, was given permission by the tsar to investigate. Rzhevsky was stopped and searched at the Finnish border en route to Christiania. The Khvostov letter was photographed, and he was allowed to continue the journey. All of Iliodor's telegrams to Khvostov were now being scrutinized by military intelligence. Rzhevsky was stopped on his return and found to have a letter from Iliodor naming three potential assassins. They were arrested and deported to their home town of Tsaritsyn.

When the tsar was informed of the plot to assassinate Rasputin, he sacked Khvostov and banished him to his estate, having first had him stripped of his decorations. Khvostov was subsequently arrested by the provisional government and held in Moscow, where the Bolsheviks eventually shot him, together with Beletsky.

Spy Mania

These events took place against a background of Russian failure at the front and a rising tide of spy mania. The military leadership was seeking a scapegoat, and the first one to hand was a Colonel Myasoyedov, who was not only close to the war minister, Vladimir Sukhomlinov, but had already faced a charge of espionage in 1912. He was arrested in January 1915 on the flimsiest of evidence and executed with lightning speed.

Rumours, created by Prince Andronnikov, a close associate of Rasputin's, began spreading that Sukhomlinov was implicated, and he was duly discharged by the tsar. The idea of 'treason in high places' was a risky policy, considering that the empress was of German origin, and indeed was being called 'the German woman'.

A safer and more traditional target was Russia's Jewish population, especially those inhabiting the area of the front. They were subjected to all kinds of persecution and atrocity, ranging from evacuation at a few hours' notice, to hanging for allegedly passing military secrets to the enemy – as Yiddish was closely related to medieval German, it was easily believed that the Jews and the Germans were in league. For instance, Jewish brothel-keepers were accused of deliberately infecting their girls with venereal disease which they in turn passed on to Russian officers. Hundreds of thousands of poor Jews were cast out of their homes without provision of any kind, wandering generally eastwards and adding to the already chaotic condition of the winter roads. Equally, prominent Jews became targets in the spy hysteria which swept the capital, along with indiscriminate accusations of pro-German sentiment that were being spread with an efficiency known only in Petrograd. Simanovich, who had more connections than were good for him, was held in custody for a brief time.

SIX

FRIENDS AND ENEMIES

Friends

A mong Rasputin's many associates, the shadiest must have been Prince Michael Andronnikov. Born of an Armenian father and German mother, by the time the war began he had established himself as a major – and utterly corrupt – contact man, with access to high society, government and banking circles, as well as senior clergy: although nominally a Lutheran, he had once held a lowly post in the Holy Synod, but knew how to cultivate the hierarchy. He was related to Princess Orbeliani, Simanovich's first patroness, and it was not long before he was introduced to his spiritual twin, Father Gregory himself.

His main tool for gaining leverage was information: he would invite the messenger-boys of important institutions to his lavish apartment, ply them with food, drink and sex – he was well known as an active homosexual – and while they were sleeping, go through their briefcases for useful information. This enabled him to insinuate that he knew about events before they occurred, for instance, being able to congratulate someone on a promotion as it happened, hinting that he had had a hand in it. In the petty-minded, self-seeking world of corrupt personal ambition that was the capital of the Russian Empire, Prince Andronnikov was the Russian con-man incarnate. Flattery and bribery, combined with detailed knowledge of an official's little weaknesses, soon made Andronnikov a rich and powerful figure. Describing himself as 'the Aide-de-Camp of Our Lord Above', he told the Provisional Government's investigation commission in 1917 that his profession was 'visiting ministers'.[1]

A lavish entertainer, Andronnikov's apartment was always full of guests – often young officers who were eventually ordered to stay away, equally often poor street boys – whom he wined and dined on costly delicacies, washed down by the best vintages. He met Rasputin early in 1914, and became closely involved in the 'saint of Tobolsk' scandal, which is described below. It was at Andronnikov's apartment in late 1914 that Rasputin was introduced to Stepan Beletsky, who had once been hostile, but was now desperate to get back into the job of deputy interior minister from which he had been dropped in 1913. He also proposed that Khvostov be appointed in place of Prince Shcherbatov, a move that, as we have seen, suited Rasputin admirably.

One of Rasputin's most valued friends was the banker Dmitri Rubinstein, a relative of the composer. They had been introduced in the spring of 1914, either by Rasputin's assistant, Simanovich, or Anna Vyrubova, whose charities he had been assisting for some time. Rubinstein was happy to give generous support to almost any charitable cause Rasputin cared to name, including some patronized by the empress. He wanted very much to receive the title of Actual State Counsellor, and with it the satisfaction of being addressed as 'Your Excellency'. In due course he was granted his dream.

It was probably in 1916 that the empress asked Rasputin to find her a trustworthy banker for a delicate task. She was happy with the suggestion of Rubinstein. The job she wanted him to do was to help her transmit funds to her poor relations in Germany, which in wartime was very difficult, though not impossible. Various clandestine forms of commerce managed to continue between Russia and Germany throughout the war, thanks largely to the survival of devious channels through Scandinavia. Rubinstein carried out the empress's commission, and she was most grateful.

Rasputin and Rubinstein tried to be useful to each other. The banker paid his rent, and Rasputin sent people in need of money or a job to Rubinstein for help, which the banker never refused. And through Rasputin's connections, Rubinstein was assured of the introductions that led to lucrative deals.

All this was known to the police. One of Rasputin's female visitors told the police in February 1916 that Rasputin had 'just arranged some matter or other for Rubinstein, the banker, who has given him fifty thousand roubles in return.'[2]

Rumours about Rubinstein's business practices were already circulating when he committed a major error: he sold his shares in the Anchor Insurance Company to a Swedish insurance firm, and with the share certificates handed over the drawings of all the buildings the company insured. At a time of hysteria about spies, all travellers and mail were being searched at the frontiers, and the inspectors thought the drawings were part of a major espionage plan. With Stuermer as a prime minister determined to live down his German name and advertise his Russian patriotism, and Rasputin ill-disposed to Rubinstein at this moment over some financial dealings, the military authorities were free to arrest him.

Other prominent Jews were arrested at this time in an attempt by the military leadership to divert blame for their failures on the field from themselves and to stoke up the spy mania. Jewish community leaders begged Simanovich to do something, and he managed to persuade Rasputin to intercede for Rubinstein. He took Rubinstein's wife to the empress, who had been badly shaken by the arrest and was fearful that her own dealings with Rubinstein would come out. She now promised to go at once to GHQ to persuade Nicholas to release Rubinstein, and, after some delay, this was done in December 1916.

Another of Rasputin's associates was Ivan

Manasevich-Manuilov, a Jew who converted to Lutheranism and who moved in high government, banking and right-wing political circles as a confidential agent. In the summer of 1916 he threatened to expose the shady dealings of a Moscow bank unless he was paid 25,000 roubles. The bank paid him in marked bills and he was duly arrested. A trial would inevitably have dragged in others, notably Rasputin, who at once turned to the empress. She told the tsar what was at stake, no doubt stressing the fact that the minister of justice, Makarov, had four years earlier been involved in the scandal concerning her letters to Rasputin: Makarov was no friend. Not only was Manuilov released without trial, but Makarov was sacked. This was blatant proof, if it were still needed, of Rasputin's enormous influence.

The *dramatis personae* of the Rasputin tragicomedy were drawn from many different levels of Russian society. Apart from the nobility and titled aristocracy, we have encountered Jewish bankers, ex-horse-thieves turned bishop, civil servants of little talent and big ambition, homosexual priests and con-men. And of course at the top of the cast list stand the tsar and tsarina.

Any notion that this widely varied group held common views of any sort would be misplaced. Their only affinity was self-interest and their unscrupulous exploitation of Rasputin to achieve their ends. Rasputin was equally unscrupulous for his own purposes, and it was only their mutual needs that held the group together. There were constant squabbles and recrimination, back-biting and back-stabbing, which, coupled with the group's greed and ambition, eventually brought about the collapse of the unholy alliance. Rasputin and Andronnikov fell out over money. Khvostov felt so confident of the tsar's support that he began to see he could manage without the liability of Rasputin's friendship, while Rasputin was soon intriguing to get rid of him.

By the beginning of 1916 it had been clear to Nicholas that his aged prime minister, Goremykin, must be replaced with someone who not only had the confidence of the other ministers – which Goremykin totally lacked – but who could also work with the Duma. Khvostov's dearest wish was to be prime minister, but Rasputin did not trust him. The alternative was not much better. In the climate of spy mania, even Boris Stuermer's

blatantly German name, which he tried
unsuccessfully to change, was a handicap. But, more
important, he was widely regarded as a third-rate
mediocrity whose appointment in January 1916
appalled almost everyone. Even Rasputin, who
engineered his appointment through his customary
route of the empress to the tsar, saw Stuermer as
only a stop-gap. But Stuermer had promised to
work with Father Gregory, and that made him
acceptable.

The collapse of Khvostov's plans led to open
conflict with his deputy, Beletsky. They threw mud
at each other in unprecedented press interviews,
and the public spectacle, together with the news
that the minister and his deputy had actually
planned an assassination, was widely seen as deeply
damaging to the throne. Nicholas got rid of
Beletsky and Khvostov, too, for good measure.
Prince Andronnikov had already been banished as a
suspect in the assassination plot.

Enemies

One of Rasputin's most powerful enemies was
Grand Duke Nikolai Nikolayevich, the tsar's cousin

and supreme commander-in-chief of the armed forces. His wife and her sister, daughters of the King of Montenegro, had brought Rasputin to the Court, and the grand duke himself had been on good terms with him. Vyrubova's emergence as the empress's confidante-in-chief drove a wedge between Alexandra and the sisters well before the war, and Rasputin had had to take sides. He chose the empress and thereby cast himself as their enemy. Their husbands became equally hostile.

Nikolai Nikolayevich, an immensely tall man of military bearing – often seen in news film and photographs towering above the diminutive figure of the tsar as they inspected the troops – was popular both in the army and with a public that saw a symbolically big man in charge of the war effort. Though no liberal, he was more flexible in his approach to political demands than his more brittle cousin. He had persuaded Nicholas to make the concessions in 1905 that had saved the regime, and he was generally perceived to represent a more vigorous part of the dynasty, enjoying the support, for example, of the dowager empress, who could not forget her late husband's disdain for Nicholas.

As supreme commander, however, Nikolai

Nikolayevich was no genius. With a seemingly inexhaustible supply of manpower, his idea of modern warfare was to throw more and more men at the enemy's artillery. Russian losses since the first battles of the war were horrific. Politically also he lacked imagination. He failed to see the damage his persecution of the Jewish population was inflicting on the Western Allies' perception of the Russian regime. Criticism, notably in the British Parliament, was reflected also in outraged American opinion, which was otherwise neutral for the time being.

The tsar, although no military man, harboured an outdated, if romantic belief that a monarch's place in war was at the head of his troops, and as Russia's defeats mounted, so his desire to command at the front grew stronger. Behind him, and pushing him towards more 'kingly' behaviour, stood his wife. Alexandra hated Grand Duke Nikolai, not only because of his hostility to her holy Friend, but also because she feared his political ambition. She firmly believed that he wanted the downfall of her husband so that he could take over and bring Russia to victory. She wanted her husband to be plainly in charge when victory came.

And behind Alexandra stood Rasputin. With Russia's fortunes sinking into the mud of the battlefield, and as criticism of the autocracy became more explicit in the Duma, Alexandra felt greater need of his spiritual support. Her confidence in the autocracy was unshaken and she believed that Rasputin could give her the spiritual strength to say so. She also believed that he could use his supernatural powers to help the tsar at this fateful hour. In July 1915, Alexandra called Rasputin back from Siberia, where he had been visiting his family. He returned at once, met the tsar the same day, and again four days later. He urged Nicholas to heed Alexandra's advice and take over the supreme command from his cousin. Once Nicholas had agreed, Rasputin left for Siberia. When the tsar departed for the front, he took with him a comb that belonged to the starets, and before he addressed the ministers he had summoned to GHQ to hear his momentous decision, he followed his wife's instructions to comb his hair with it to reinforce his resolve.

The ministers were appalled by the tsar's decision, sensing the huge risk involved in his taking over when the country's military fortunes were so low. They also saw that, with Nicholas away at the front, his wife's influence on affairs of state, and therefore that of Rasputin, would be greatly enhanced. Apart from the senile prime minister, Ivan Goremykin, and two or three other ministers, the entire administration signed a letter of protest to Nicholas, offering their resignations if he insisted on replacing the grand duke. He would not allow them to resign.

Before the war, Alexandra had limited her role in high politics to getting rid of anyone who attacked Rasputin. Now, she was closely involved on a day-to-day basis. Her son's French tutor, Pierre Gilliard, had many opportunities to study her closely. He saw in her an artistic and well-educated woman who enjoyed reading and the arts, and who was prone to introspection, from which she would emerge when danger threatened, at which point she would throw herself at the obstacle with all the ardour of her passionate nature. She had the highest moral qualities, but the sadness of her life, after the birth of the heir and with the mounting opposition to the autocracy, had broken her. She was a shadow of her former self, and she often had periods of mystic ecstasy in which she lost all sense of reality. Her faith in Rasputin, as Gilliard correctly points out, proved this beyond doubt.

She wanted her husband to stand on the military pedestal; Rasputin had always urged the tsar, either face to face or through her, to stand up to the opposition; together they had virtually conspired to give Nicholas his wish. The grand duke was sent to command the troops in the Caucasus, and Nicholas, who had no military experience, acquired the highly competent General Alexeev as his chief of staff.

Before Nicholas could address himself to military affairs, however, a new scandal struck. Rasputin's old partner in crime, Barnaby, who had been made bishop of Tobolsk, had been planning the canonization of a certain John Maximilianovich, a seventeenth-century Metropolitan of Tobolsk who had forcibly baptized the population of Siberia. Local saints were very good for business, and Barnaby had Rasputin's vigorous support in this venture, as well as that of the empress.

Rasputin sent a telegram to Nicholas only three days after he had taken over supreme command, urging him to overrule the Holy Synod, which was dragging its feet, and to order the canonization. Even before Alexandra had cabled her own support, the tsar had given permission for Barnaby to pronounce preliminary sainthood, thus overriding the Holy Synod and most of Church opinion. The director of the Holy Synod, Alexander Samarin, was sacked, and as he was a popular figure in his native Moscow, his fall added fuel to the already restless political élite of that city, who, however loyal they might be to the tsar, saw this latest affront as a political act inspired by Rasputin and his clique. According to one of its most astute observers, the Samarin scandal had made the Moscow nobility into 'a hotbed of revolution'.[3]

When Metropolitan Flavian of Petrograd died in November 1915, Rasputin manoeuvred to secure the post for his old friend, Pitirim, a homosexual hierarch with a record of corruption and immorality that would have sunk any other churchman. Rasputin and Alexandra urged the tsar to overrule the Holy Synod, all of whose voting members wanted nothing of Pitirim, and the deed was done. It was later claimed that Rasputin had received 75,000 roubles from Pitirim for his patronage. This was more than recouped by Pitirim who apparently siphoned off 100,466 roubles from his monastery's funds in 1916 alone.

Meanwhile, Rasputin and Pitirim set out to purge the Church hierarchy of their enemies by ruthlessly exploiting Alexandra's friendship. In doing so, they were miring the dynasty still further in disrepute and bad judgement. Samarin was replaced by Alexander Volzhin, who tried to ensure his success by accommodating the demands of Rasputin or his friends. Barnaby's local 'saint' was fully canonized in June 1916 and Barnaby himself was made archbishop in October, while other senior positions in the Holy Synod were secured for men friendly to Father Gregory. At all levels of the hierarchy, illiterate, ignorant, corrupt and discredited priests were given good positions because they had Rasputin's support.

The situation was so scandalous that in November 1916 it was debated in the Duma, where the influence of Rasputin and his followers was described as 'an ulcer that threatens to infect the whole of the church organism',[4] and might even cause a total split resulting in the formation of another church.

It was mostly right-wing, monarchist and conservative opinion that was exercised over these developments. The liberal intelligentsia was too broad in its philosophies to hold a common view: many were indifferent to the internal difficulties of an institution they regarded as primitive and outmoded, while others found a natural affinity between the Church's social teaching and the liberal goal of the just society. For Marxists, the very existence of the Church, like all other religious bodies, was merely further evidence of the need for socialist revolution: the eradication of a church that kept the people ignorant and passive, that preached consolation only in the next world, could not come soon enough.

Nicholas had decided it would be good for morale if he took the tsarevich with him to the front, and he was probably right. The sight of the eleven-year-old boy, in his private's uniform, alongside the tsar, proved to be a good public relations move, even though the empress was understandably nervous for the boy's health, and in time also for his neglected education. Whatever benefit the tsar's image may have derived, however, was overshadowed by the mounting public indignation at Rasputin's apparently unlimited powers.

Society saw that Rasputin could sack ministers,

create bishops, archbishops, a metropolitan and a saint, and even get rid of the supreme commander. His power, or that of those he chose to sponsor, seemed absolute.

Rasputin was careful in what he said about politics. His network at Court ensured that he was always up to date on the current mood, on who was in, who was out, so that to a large extent his prophecies, when he gave them, tended to confirm Alexandra's own desires. Hearing them from his infallible lips, she felt that they had the authority of revelation.

SEVEN

THE END

Ministerial Leapfrog

Since taking over supreme command in the summer of 1915, Nicholas had left the handling of his ministers to his wife who, as had been predicted, would exercise her new powers under the 'spiritual guidance' of her powerful friend, Rasputin. It is important to note that Rasputin was being called upon to employ his healing powers over the tsarevich only very rarely now. He had established himself as a 'courtier', with his own network of cronies and associates, and it was this role, enhanced in Alexandra's eyes by his spiritual infallibility, that gave him his power.

Meanwhile, influential Duma deputies were constantly demanding that Nicholas should appoint a government with which they could collaborate, one that enjoyed their confidence, one that would join its own efforts with the industrial and other contributions the Duma and its supporters could make to the war effort.

The tsar's idea of co-operation with the Duma, however, was that it should work harder to facilitate his policies, that it should cease its constant criticism and show loyalty and allegiance. For almost all shades of political opinion in the Duma – apart from the extreme right wing which was illogically hostile to the whole concept of a democratically elected legislature – co-operation meant sharing responsibilities, and joint participation in policy making and execution. The very idea was deeply repugnant to the empress, who pushed Nicholas hard to resist the Duma's demands.

Meanwhile, in the search for strong and reliable men to run the government, she engaged in a such a welter of ministerial appointments that Nicholas complained that they made his head spin. Between September 1915 and March 1917, there were four prime ministers, five interior ministers, four agriculture ministers, three war ministers and a host of others, some holding office for less than two months.

Not all of these appointments depended on

Rasputin's patronage. Indeed, it is important to note that only the tsar had the power to appoint and dismiss ministers, and that Alexandra's role was advisory. On occasion, Nicholas not only resisted her recommendations, but even reminded her that 'our Friend's opinions of people are sometimes very strange.'[1] In the appointment of Alexander Protopopov as interior minister in September 1916, however, he succumbed to the heavy pressure that Rasputin was exerting through Alexandra. Protopopov was a Duma deputy from the moderate Octobrist party and his appointment was consciously designed by Alexandra and Rasputin as a sop to the Duma.

The idea that Protopopov was going to save Russia was quickly dashed. The winter of 1916 saw an improvement in the condition of the Russian army, thanks at least partly to the efforts of the various public bodies, which under the auspices of the Duma had been helping to organize war production. But the condition of the home front was worsening and becoming critical. Food, fuel supply and distribution had been severely disrupted by the mobilization: the Russian army was mostly made up of 'peasants in soldiers' greatcoats'. And the army naturally took the lion's share of all the food produced, while it also absorbed most of the country's transport resources.

Inflation was rampant, the value of the rouble plummeted, and rationing had been introduced in the summer of 1916. Rasputin believed that the cities could be fed if responsibility was taken out of the hands of the agriculture minister and given to the interior minister, who could then use police powers to ensure fair play. It is amazing that the government itself did not take such a rational step much earlier.

The tsar backed this idea, against the judgement of most of the other ministers, but at the crucial moment Protopopov – who deserves credit for recognizing his own limitations – begged to be allowed to share the responsibility with two other ministers. The royal couple were disappointed, while Rasputin was furious, though he did not abandon Protopopov; perhaps there was not enough time for him to do so. Protopopov meanwhile consulted his astrologer for guidance and resorted to Dr Badmaev's clinic to benefit from his Tibetan herbs when the stress proved too great.

With the tsar and his wife now so patently

isolated from the political establishment, and the government so utterly discredited as a creature of the scheming 'holy man', the situation in Russia in the winter of 1916 was truly at crisis point. In a speech to the Duma in November, Paul Milyukov, the moderate leader of the liberal Constitutional Democrats, catalogued the government's failures, rhetorically concluding each point with the inflammatory question, 'Is this treason or stupidity?' As the empress was now commonly being called 'the German woman', the implications were clear. Ironically, even Rasputin believed the situation was hopeless, that Russia was being governed by fools, and that both the tsar and tsarina had lost their way, their will and their judgement. He predicted disaster.

The Murder of Rasputin

Prince Felix Yusupov was in his way almost as enigmatic a character as Rasputin, whose murder he plotted and carried out in December 1916. He was the immensely wealthy son of Russia's richest family, and was married to the extraordinarily beautiful Princess Irina, the tsar's only niece. He himself was described as the most beautiful man in Russia.

After three happy years as an undergraduate at Oxford, he had spent a further year as one of the most lavish bachelor hosts in London society. He had contemplated marriage with the daughter of an English duke, whose other daughter had wanted to marry him, and in 1913, after returning home to St Petersburg, he had decided to marry Irina. There was resistance from Irina's parents, and the empress, too, when they heard that Felix was notoriously homosexual. But Irina was under-standing, and he managed to persuade the others that the misdemeanours of his youth were a thing of the past, and that now he was 'straight'. The couple were duly wed in February 1914.

Homosexuality was a serious crime in Russia, punishable by exile at least. But being a member of the aristocracy had many benefits, one of which was the blind eye turned by the state to this particular transgression. Felix's sexual orientation had been unclear since early childhood. At the age of twelve in France, through a window he had witnessed a couple making love, and claimed in his memoirs that the man, an Argentinian, arranged for him to watch a repeat performance at close quarters. He found the scene so overpowering that he was at first 'unable to discriminate between the sexes.'[2] As a child he had loved dressing up as a girl and by this time was a confirmed transvestite. He became a practising homosexual in his teenage years.

Before going up to Oxford, he had experienced a spiritual crisis. His conscience was deeply stirred by the contrast between his own lavish lifestyle and that of the rest of the people in the country, especially the most poverty-stricken. Wearing beggar's clothing, he saw for himself the indescribable squalor of the lower depths in Russia's richest cities, St Petersburg and Moscow. In a fit of noble-minded repentance, he determined to sell off the Yusupov assets and to build hospitals and old people's homes with the proceeds, and to open the family's palaces to the public. His mother urged that his higher duty was to preserve the family fortune for its own posterity, and he took little persuading. The religious feeling that was stirred up in him at this time, however, appears to have been genuine enough, and it added a touch of mysticism to his otherwise purely hedonistic character.

When war broke out, Felix – who was exempt

from military service as an only son, his elder brother having been killed in a duel before the war – converted his enormous palace in the capital into a military hospital, and enrolled in the Cadet Corps for the sake of appearances. In March 1915, Irina gave birth to a daughter, and joy reigned in the family. Three months later, anti-German riots in Moscow, where Felix's father was governor-general, got out of control and Yusupov Senior was ignominiously dismissed. Felix's mother was convinced that Rasputin and the tsarina had conspired to bring about this humiliating situation, and she wrote to her son in this vein.

As was true of most other noble families, the Yusupovs were deeply concerned by the effect Rasputin's influence was having on the Romanov dynasty. Now, they became sworn enemies, and Felix's mother believed both the starets and Alexandra ought somehow to be set aside.

Felix may have been genuinely alarmed at the political consequences of the situation and decided to kill Gregory out of a sense of public duty, but his distaste for the unsavoury starets was first aroused in 1909, when he met him at the Golovins. His refined sensibilities were so deeply offended by the sight of the disgusting muzhik kissing the beautiful young and innocent Munia Golovina on the lips that he wanted to crush him like an insect. He may have been so bored with his life of plenty that only by committing a sensational crime could he find excitement.

It was widely believed that the tsar as supreme commander was carrying out policy only with Rasputin's prior approval, which was wholly wrong. In practice, Nicholas urged his wife not to discuss military affairs with Gregory, but the public at large, and even the well-informed, did not know this. The mere idea that Rasputin was seeing the tsarina regularly and that she was running the government was enough to convince everyone that Russia's war effort was being seriously undermined by 'dark forces' headed by the 'German woman', who was herself manipulated by the 'holy devil'.

It has also been suggested that Yusupov's fascination with Rasputin was not hostile, but was based on homosexual attraction, some say requited, others rejected. He is also reported to have first gone to see Gregory to be cured of his condition, which evidently gave him great spiritual anguish and guilt. Alternatively, there is a theory that this was merely a ploy to win Rasputin's trust so that the murder could be more easily planned. Moreover, so many people declared that Rasputin must be disposed of that Felix saw he would not be alone, and that killing Rasputin would be greeted as an act of public heroism and patriotic sacrifice.

In this state of mind, he went to see opposition Duma Deputy Vasili Maklakov in the belief that he would help find an assassin. Maklakov thought the plan was futile, because Rasputin would soon be replaced. Felix was adamant that this could not happen, because a man with Rasputin's supernatural powers was a rarity. 'If he were killed today,' he argued, 'the Empress would go to a home for nervous disorders within a fortnight and Nicholas would become a constitutional monarch.'[3] Maklakov remained uncommitted, but promised legal help, if necessary.

Felix then found Vladimir Purishkevich. A rabidly right-wing, anti-Semitic deputy in a Duma whose very purpose he despised, Purishkevich was perhaps the best-known Russian politician. He revelled in shocking behaviour, showing his contempt for the political process by, for instance, appearing in the Chamber with a bright red carnation sticking out of his flies. He published scurrilous and satirical lampoons, and he hated Rasputin as a malignancy at the heart of the Russian state. A few days after Milyukov's powerful 'treason or stupidity' speech, Purishkevich delivered a blistering attack on the 'dark forces . . . headed by Grishka Rasputin', and called on the Duma to raise its voice to urge the tsar that 'Grishka Rasputin be not the leader of Russian internal public life.'[4]

Prince Yusupov was in the parliament when Purishkevich made his speech, and was sufficiently stirred to call on him two days later to tell him of his plan to murder the starets. Purishkevich agreed at once to join the plot, proposing a friend, Dr Stanislaus Lazovert, as a valuable ally and physician who could supply poison.

Felix then turned to his lifelong friend, possibly former lover, certainly one-time rival for the hand of Irina, Grand Duke Dmitri Pavlovich, a close relative of Nicholas, now the tsar's aide and an ardent enemy of Rasputin. He was firmly of the belief that Rasputin was using drugs to keep Nicholas in a state of passive compliance.

The fourth conspirator was a friend of Yusupov's, a young lieutenant called Ivan Sukhotin. In a second conversation with Vasili Maklakov, Yusupov was advised that the murderers should make sure the body was found, or the point of the assassination would be lost. Maklakov gave the prince a heavy rubber-clad club to use, if necessary, and repeated his promise to act as defence counsel, should he be needed.

Felix Yusupov was visiting Rasputin at his apartment frequently at this time, possibly every day, and the plan was to reciprocate the hospitality by inviting him to meet Felix's wife, Irina – for the first time, be it noted – on 29 December, the first available date in Grand Duke Dmitri's diary. Felix would give the starets cakes and wine laced with potassium cyanide, and then the others would take the body, wrapped up, in Purishkevich's car to a place they had found on the river where a hole in the ice was large enough for the body to be stuffed through. It would then be swept out into the Gulf of Finland and not found until the spring thaw. Maklakov's advice to ensure its discovery was evidently ignored, although this came to be of no importance. The dead man's clothes would be burnt, and a call to his favourite night spot, to ask if he had arrived yet, would establish an alibi of sorts for the conspirators at the Yusupov palace.

Yusupov and his friends, however, were not professional revolutionaries who understood the basic codes of conspiracy, and it was not long before Petrograd society knew fairly well what was going on. Rasputin, too, felt that something was brewing, but his second sight was not sharp enough for him to define precisely what. At his last meeting with the tsar, he declined to bless Nicholas, commenting, 'This time it is for you to bless me, not I you.'[5]

In a mood of impending doom, a few days before the 'party' at Yusupov's, Rasputin wrote the tsar a long letter, entitled 'The Spirit of Gregory Yefimovich Rasputin of the village of Pokrovskoe'. He predicted he would die by 1 January 1917: 'If I am killed by common assassins . . . especially peasants,' the tsar and his children would have nothing to fear and would reign for hundreds of years. 'But if I am murdered by . . . nobles . . . if it was your relations who have wrought my death, then . . . none of your children or relations will remain alive more than two years. They will be killed by the Russian people . . . I shall be killed, I am no longer among the living.'[6] It was a startlingly accurate prediction.

Yusupov spent the day supervising the preparation of a basement room to make it look lived in. Well away from the rest of the palace, whatever was to happen here was not supposed to be heard elsewhere. At midnight, the other plotters arrived, and Dr Lazovert laced the cakes and wine with enough poison to kill several people, he assured his friends. As arranged, Yusupov then left to collect Rasputin by car. They arrived back at the Yusupov Palace at 1 a.m., their entire journey tailed by one of the police agents on duty at Rasputin's apartment building.

Only Purishkevich and Yusupov wrote eye-witness accounts of the event, both of them containing contradictory detail. An extensive police report and other testimony suggest that there may have been more people involved than either of the chief witnesses was prepared to admit, and that there was a variation in the order of events. Be that as it may, the essential facts of the case are fairly clear.

As arranged, when the 'guest of honour' was heard arriving, Purishkevich and the others played a gramophone record – it was 'Yankee Doodle Dandy', Yusupov's only one. To Gregory's enquiry as to who else was in the house, Felix replied that Irina was entertaining some friends and that they would be leaving shortly. Rasputin did not know, as the empress could have informed him, that Irina was in fact in the Crimea, where she had been for some time. He was persuaded to try the cakes, which he normally never ate, and then some of the wine, followed by his favourite – poisoned – Madeira. Rasputin appeared unaffected, except to say he felt sleepy and that his throat was burning. He requested more Madeira to soothe it. Nothing happened. Whether the poison had lost its potency or been wrongly administered, it had not done its job.

Felix left the room with the excuse of finding his wife. It was by now 2 a.m. and if Rasputin did not smell a rat it seemed he never would. At the very least, he should have wondered why Irina had not appeared by now. Upstairs, the others told Felix to go back and that the poison must soon work. If it did not do its job in five minutes, he was to return for new instructions. Back in the basement, it took no more than a cup of tea to revive Rasputin who persuaded a very nervous Felix to sing gypsy songs and play his guitar. This the distraught prince allegedly did for about an hour. In desperation he then went upstairs to his friends who sent him back with Grand Duke Dmitri's Browning revolver.

Rasputin was again drowsy and complaining of burning in the stomach. He drank some more poisoned wine and seemed again somewhat revived, and, according to Yusupov, he even suggested they should go to hear the gypsies. There may actually have been two young women at the palace, but the story is vague about this. In any case, now on the verge of nervous collapse, Felix claims he said it was too late. Then, as if to counter Rasputin's demonic powers of survival, Felix invoked the force of a magnificent crystal crucifix, telling his victim to say a prayer before it. At this moment, he pulled out the revolver and shot Rasputin in the chest. The others, hearing the noise, dashed downstairs. Lazovert examined Rasputin and pronounced him dead. At 3 a.m. the assassins left the 'dead' man where he was and went upstairs to carry on with the plan. Grand Duke Dmitri, Dr Lazovert and Lieutenant Sukhotin took away Rasputin's clothes to burn them, while

Purishkevich, contentedly smoking a cigar, waited for them at the palace.

Felix, meanwhile, returned to the basement, 'drawn by an irresistible impulse.'[7] Seized by what seems like a necrophiliac fit, he later described how he had grabbed and shaken the dead body, only for Rasputin's eyes to snap open giving the prince a look of 'diabolical hatred'.[8] The 'dead' man then leapt up and went for the prince's throat. Yusupov, now possessed by a strength he had never known, tore himself free and dashed in terror up the stairs, where Purishkevich, aroused by the terrified screams – whether Yusupov's or Rasputin's – watched in horror as Rasputin, foaming at the mouth, was pursuing Felix on all fours.

Yusupov dashed past Purishkevich to his parents' apartments, while Rasputin managed to get out of the house and was now running across the courtyard, yelling 'Felix, Felix, I'll tell the Tsarina!'[9] Purishkevich fired his revolver at the departing figure, missing twice but hitting him in the back with his third shot, and in the head with a fourth, then kicking him violently in the head until it was obvious he really was dead. Purishkevich then informed the two soldiers on guard duty at the gate that he had killed Grishka Rasputin, and that they should say nothing for the sake of the tsar and country. They agreed.

Felix meanwhile, having run from another exit around the house to cut Rasputin off, should he manage to get out, entered the courtyard at another point, where a policeman who had heard the shots asked him what was going on. Yusupov explained that it was just one of his tipsy friends firing off his gun in the air.

Rasputin's body had been brought back into the house by the sentries when Yusupov, again seized by a fit of violent outrage, took the heavy club that Maklakov had given him and, screaming his own name, 'Felix, Felix', battered the head and chest of the corpse, while the others watched in stunned disbelief. It has been suggested that Felix was also experiencing a pathological sexual urge which he expressed by allegedly castrating the corpse. Vomiting, fainting, covered with his victim's blood, and totally out of control, Felix was finally carried away to rest. Dostoyevsky himself could not have composed a more grotesque or unreal scenario.

The body was then wrapped in a heavy curtain and tied up. Then Purishkevich, Grand Duke

Dmitri, Lieutenant Sukhotin and Dr Lazovert took it by car to the river. There they tossed the body over the bridge, forgetting to attach the heavy chains and weights they had planned to use to make it sink. Instead they attached these to the coat and boots that had proved too difficult to burn and threw them in. One of the boots was left by mistake on the bridge, and this was the clue that led to the discovery of the body three days later. The autopsy showed water in the lungs, proving that Rasputin had actually survived poisoning, shooting, heavy beating and possibly castration, and had died by drowning.

EIGHT

POSTSCRIPT

Despite the conspirators' denials of complicity – and Purishkevich's retraction of his admission to the police – practically the whole of Petrograd society knew who had murdered Rasputin. Their guilt was in any case quickly established by the investigation ordered by the tsar: during the shooting there were police witnesses close by. Grand Duke Dmitri's royal connection saved the group from serious punishment: Dmitri himself was posted to Persia, Yusupov was banished to one of his estates in central Russia, and Purishkevich was given a written reprimand.

The tsarina was devastated by the murder of her martyred saint, while the tsar, although shaken, was more disturbed by the fact that his own relatives could have gone so far as to commit murder. Society regarded the murderers as heroes who had saved Russia, while the peasants fatalistically accepted that Rasputin – a muzhik of muzhiks – had been got rid of by the nobility because he had been able to tell the tsar the truth about the plight of the simple folk.

His long-suffering widow, Praskovia, wanted Gregory's body brought to Pokrovskoe for burial, but she was overruled by Alexandra who had him buried at Tsarskoe Selo on 4 January 1917 in the presence of the entire royal family and Rasputin's two daughters. In March, after the fall of the monarchy, soldiers were ordered, seemingly by the new government, to dig up the body and burn it.

*

Those who had wished for the removal of Rasputin, and those who had murdered him, had been too slow to carry out the deed for it to have the desired effect. The authority of the tsar and his government had been draining away for far too long for the desperate act of Yusupov and his friends to reverse the trend. Moreover, by the winter of 1916 other factors were acting to alter the course of Russian history, factors which were outside the framework of the Rasputin story.

Cooperation between the army command and

Duma organizations had improved the supply and
equipment situation at the front; for the first time in
the war the Allies and Russia were planning a
simultaneous spring offensive in 1917 that would at
last take advantage of the fact that Germany was
having to face its enemies on two fronts; the food
and fuel position in the country at large was so dire
that strikes and demonstrations, when they
occurred in late February, would quickly get beyond
the government's control.

Undoubtedly, Rasputin had been closely involved
in the tsar's becoming isolated from his ministers
and especially from the army command. Even
though Nicholas had not allowed him to discuss
military affairs – nor did he – the perception that he
interfered in all spheres of administration was
firmly rooted. The army command was ready by
February to shift its allegiance to another tsar who
was less compromised. When a deputation from the
Duma suggested to Nicholas that he abdicate, and
when none of his generals came to his support, he
knew it was time to go. At first he wanted his sick
son to succeed him, and then thought better of it.
His brother, Michael, would have known how to
cooperate with the Duma, but the more radical,

republican elements would not guarantee his safety. He therefore declined the throne, and the Romanov dynasty slipped into history.

Rasputin's prophecy, that if he were killed by nobles the Romanovs would all be drowned in blood within two years, was fulfilled in July 1918, when the tsar and his wife, his four daughters and his son, were shot to death in another basement, that of a merchant called Ipatiev, known by its new Bolshevik masters as the House of Special Purpose, in Tobolsk, the nearest large town to Pokrovskoe, birthplace of the Romanovs' holy Friend and Nemesis, Gregory Rasputin.

NOTES

CHAPTER ONE

1. Quoted in D. Volkogonov, *Trotsky: The Eternal Revolutionary*, edited and translated H. Shukman (London, HarperCollins, 1996, paperback 1997), p. 38.

CHAPTER TWO

1. M. Rasputin, *My Father* (London, Cassell, 1934), p. 42.
2. M. Paléologue, *La Russie des Tsars pendant la Grande Guerre*, vol. 1, (Paris, Plon, 1921–2), p. 308.
3. A. Simanovich, *Rasputin i Evrei*, no place given, 1928, reprinted Tashkent, 1990), p. 16.

CHAPTER THREE

1. Cited in C. Omessa, *Rasputin and the Russian Court*, translated by Frances Keyzer (London, George Newnes, 1918), pp. 45–6.
2. A. Simanovich, *Rasputin i Evrei* (Slovo, n.p., 1928, reprint Tashkent, 1990), p. 19.
3. M. Rasputin, *My Father* (London, Cassell, 1934), p. 67.
4. M. Rasputin, *My Father* (London, Cassell, 1934), p. 64.
5. Quoted in D. Lieven, *Nicholas II: Emperor of All the Russias* (London, John Murray, 1993), p. 167.
6. M. Rodzianko, *The Reign of Rasputin,* translated by C.E. Zvegintzoff (London, A.M. Philpot, 1927), p. 24.
7. Quoted in R. Massie, *Nicholas and Alexandra* (New York, Atheneum, 1967), p. 199.

CHAPTER FOUR

1. Cited in M. Rasputin, *My Father* (London, Cassell, 1934), p. 72.

Notes

CHAPTER FIVE

1. Quoted in J.T. Fuhrmann, *Rasputin: A Life* (New York, Praeger, 1990), p. 108.

2. Cited in D. Lieven, *Nicholas II: Emperor of All the Russias* (London, John Murray, 1993), p. 168.

3. Quoted in A. de Jonge, *The Life and Times of Grigorii Rasputin* (London, Collins, 1982), p. 240.

4. Quoted in J.T. Fuhrmann, *Rasputin: A Life* (New York, Praeger, 1990), p. 120.

5. Quoted in A. de Jonge, *The Life and Times of Grigorii Rasputin* (London, Collins, 1982), p. 262.

6. Quoted in A. de Jonge, *The Life and Times of Grigorii Rasputin* (London, Collins, 1982), p. 263.

7. A. Simanovich, *Rasputin i Evrei* (n.p., 1928, reprint Tashkent, 1990), p. 82.

8. A. Simanovich, *Rasputin i Evrei* (n.p., 1928, reprint Tashkent, 1990), p. 82.

CHAPTER SIX

1. Quoted in G. Katkov, *Russia: 1917* (London, Longman, 1967), p. 209.

2. R. Fülöp-Miller, *Rasputin, The Holy Devil*, translated from the German by F.S. Flint and D.F. Tait (New York, Viking Press, 1928), p, 185.

3. Princess Paley, cited in J.T. Fuhrmann, *Rasputin: A Life* (New York, Praeger, 1990), p. 138.

4. J.T. Fuhrmann, *Rasputin: A Life* (New York, Praeger, 1990), p. 156.

CHAPTER SEVEN

1. Quoted in J.T. Fuhrmann, *Rasputin: A Life* (New York, Praeger, 1990), p. 180.

2. F. Youssoupoff, *Avant l'Exil* (Paris, Plon, 1952), p. 41.

3. A. de Jonge, *The Life and Times of Grigorii Rasputin* (London, Collins, 1982), p. 310.

4. A. de Jonge, *The Life and Times of Grigorii Rasputin* (London,

Notes

Collins, 1982), pp. 312–13.

5. G. King, *The Murder of Rasputin* (London, Arrow Books, 1997), p. 145.

6. G. King, *The Murder of Rasputin* (London, Arrow Books, 1997), p. 146.

7. F. Youssoupoff, *Avant l'Exil* (Paris, Plon, 1952), p. 246.

8. Quoted in D. Napley, *Rasputin in Hollywood* (London, Weidenfeld and Nicolson, 1989), p. 7.

9. V. Purishkevich, *Dnevnik* (National Reklama, Riga, 1924), p. 80.

BIBLIOGRAPHY

Publishers' location is London, unless stated otherwise.

J.T. Fuhrmann, *Rasputin: A Life*, New York, Praeger, 1990

R. Fülöp-Miller, *Rasputin, The Holy Devil*, translated from the German by F.S. Flint and D.F. Tait, New York, Viking Press, 1928

Pierre Gilliard, *Thirteen Years at the Russian Court*, translated by F. Appleby Holt, Bath, Cedric Chivers, 1972

A. de Jonge, *The Life and Times of Grigorii Rasputin*, Collins, 1982

G. Katkov, *Russia 1917: The February Revolution*, Longman, 1967

G. King, *The Murder of Rasputin*, Century, 1996, and Arrow Books, 1997

D. Lieven, *Nicholas II: Emperor of All the Russias*, John Murray, 1993

D. Napley, *Rasputin in Hollywood*, Weidenfeld and Nicolson, 1989

C. Omessa, *Rasputin and the Russian Court*, translated by Frances Keyzer, George Newnes, 1918

M. Paléologue, *La Russie des Tsars pendant la Grande Guerre*, vol. 1, Paris, Plon-Nourrit et Cie, 1921–2

Maria Rasputin, *My Father*, Cassell, 1934

M. Rodzianko, *The Reign of Rasputin*, translated by C.E. Zvegintzoff, A.M. Philpot, 1927

Bibliography

H. Shukman, *The Blackwell Encyclopedia of the Russian Revolution*, Oxford, Blackwell, 1988

A. Simanovich, *Rasputin i Evrei*, no place of publication given, 1928, reprinted Tashkent, 1990

D. Volkogonov, *Trotsky: The Eternal Revolutionary*, edited and translated by H. Shukman, HarperCollins, 1996, paperback 1997

F. Youssoupoff, *Avant l'Exil*, Paris, Plon, 1952

POCKET BIOGRAPHIES

This series looks at the lives of those who have played a significant part in our history – from musicians to explorers, from scientists to entertainers, from writers to philosophers, from politicians to monarchs throughout the world. Concise and highly readable, with black and white plates, chronology and bibliography, these books will appeal to students and general readers alike.

Available

Beethoven
Anne Pimlott Baker

Mao Zedong
Delia Davin

Scott of the Antarctic
Michael De-la-Noy

Alexander the Great
E.E. Rice

Sigmund Freud
Stephen Wilson

Marilyn Monroe
Sheridan Morley and
Ruth Leon

Jane Austen
Helen Lefroy

POCKET BIOGRAPHIES

Forthcoming

Marie and Pierre Curie
John Senior

Ellen Terry
Moira Shearer

David Livingstone
Christine Nicholls

Margot Fonteyn
Alistair Macauley

Winston Churchill
Robert Blake

Abraham Lincoln
H.G. Pitt

Charles Dickens
Catherine Peters

Enid Blyton
George Greenfield